There is one who makes himself rich,

yet has nothing;

And one who makes himself poor,

yet has great riches.

PROVERBS 13:7

Empty at the Top

ATHENA DEAN HOLTZ

Empty AT THE TOP

Exposing Spiritual Dangers in Multilevel Marketing

REDEMPTION PRESS

Originally titled *Consumed by Success*, published by WinePress Publishing—1995

Second printing, August 1996

Third printing, revised, expanded, updated and retitled, published by Redemption Press—2023

Copyright © Athena Dean Holtz

All rights reserved. No part of this publication may be reproduced, stored in a retrieval system, or transmitted in any way by any means, electronic, mechanical, photocopy, recording or otherwise, without the prior permission of the publisher, except as provided by USA copyright law.

Unless otherwise indicated, all Scripture quotations are taken from the New King James Version of the Bible. Copyright © 1979, 1980, 1982, Thomas Nelson, Inc., Publishers.

Scripture quotations marked (NIV) are taken from THE HOLY BIBLE, NEW INTERNATIONAL VERSION®, NIV® Copyright © 1973, 1978, 1984, 2011 by Biblica, Inc.® Used by permission. All rights reserved worldwide.

Scripture quotations marked (AMP) Are taken from the Amplified Bible, Copyright © 2015 by The Lockman Foundation, La Habra, CA 90631. All rights reserved.

Scripture quotations marked (ESV) are taken from The ESV® Bible (The Holy Bible, English Standard Version®), copyright © 2001 by Crossway, a publishing ministry of Good News Publishers. Used by permission. All rights reserved.

Scriptures marked NAS are taken from the *New American Standard* (NAS): Scripture taken from the *New American Standard Bible*® Copyright© 1960, 1971, 1972, 1973, 1975, 1977, 1995 by The Lockman Foundation. Used by permission.

Unless otherwise indicated, all Scripture quotations are taken from *The Living Bible* (TLB,) Copyright© 1971 by Tyndale House Foundation. Used by permission of Tyndale House Publishers Inc., Carol Stream, Illinois 60188. All rights reserved.

Unless otherwise indicated, all Scripture quotations are taken from the *Amplified Bible* (AMP) *or the Amplified Bible, Classic Edition* (AMPC,) Copyright© 1954, 1958, 1962, 1964, 1965, 1987 by the Lockman Foundation. Used by Permission. (www.Lockan.org)

Scripture marked (KJV) are taken from the *King James Version* (KJV): *King James Version*, public domain.

Scripture quotations marked (NLT) are taken from the *Holy Bible*, New Living Translation, copyright © 1996, 2004, 2015 by Tyndale House Foundation. Used by permission of Tyndale House Publishers, Inc., Carol Stream, Illinois 60188. All rights reserved.

Printed in the United States of America

Softcover: 978-1-951310-86-8
ePub: 978-1-951310-87-5
Audiobook: 978-1-951310-88-2
Library of Congress Catalog Card Number: 2023904762

DEDICATION

While most of this content is almost thirty years old,
nothing has really changed in the pursuit of the American Dream.
However, I am no longer married to the person this story includes.
I am grateful for the support my pastor husband, Dr. Ross Holtz,
has given me as I've reshaped the material to bring light
to a murky deception that is still running rampant
in the church in America.

ACKNOWLEDGMENTS

Special thanks go to my children, Aaron, Garrett, Ailen, and Roby, for putting up with a mother who was consumed for so many years. I know I've said it before, but I'm sorry. I love you guys!

Much appreciation also goes to Inger Logelin for her diligence and commitment in the original and second editing process, and to Kathy Ide for her insightful help on the third edition. And to my husband, Ross, who read this for feedback and clarity. It has definitely been refined thanks to these three people. I could never have done this without all of you!

And finally, thank you to all those online and across the country who shared their stories with me. While many of them were heartbreaking, they dramatically illustrate a problem we can no longer ignore.

CONTENTS

Acknowledgments		ix
Introduction		xiii
Prologue		xv
1.	It's Not What You Have, It's What Has You	17
2.	Looking for Love in All the Wrong Places	27
3.	It All Sounded So Good!	37
4.	God's Idea or Good Idea?	43
5.	Doing the Wrong Thing for the Right Reason	51
6.	Fatal Attractions	61
7.	Selling the Dream	67
8.	Miracle Workers and False Profits	83
9.	It All Came Crashing Down	91
10.	The Blinding Lights of Success	107
11.	Body Count in the Church	115
12.	Have We Been Robbed?	127
13.	You Can Be Free from the Trap	143
14.	The Narrow Way	153
Epilogue		161
Endnotes		167
Suggested Reading		169
Other Resources by Athena Dean Holtz		170

INTRODUCTION

It's been a little less than thirty years since the first edition of this material came out. Under the title *Consumed by Success: Reaching the Top and Finding God Wasn't There*, I took a brave stand against the multilevel marketing business model. Lately God has been nudging me to get that book updated and back into print.

Reading the words I penned all those years ago brought back a flood of emotions. During that time, God gave me many insights as I came to realize how deceived I had been in my stride to reach the top of three different network marketing organizations. Even though I experienced great success monetarily, I could not deny the Scriptures that brought my house of cards tumbling down.

Too many times during those years, I responded to the lack of money with bright ideas to make more. When funds dried up, I became vulnerable to the deception of the enemy of my soul to find a way out through compromising my beliefs.

Today I run a successful publishing business founded on godly principles instead of the "get rich quick" schemes I fell prey to for so many years. Yet even now, during the occasional seasons when revenue dips, a potential manuscript comes in that would be a compromise to publish. Either the content is doctrinally inaccurate or it contains a message I cannot in good conscience endorse. Still, temptation arises. The enemy would love for me to let my guard down and take the easy way out instead of trusting the Lord to provide.

I believe when God allows us to experience a period of financial drought, He wants us to come to Him and surrender, open to what He may be saying to our hearts, instead of running ahead of Him and coming up with our own solutions.

When I was first approached with an opportunity to buy into the "American Dream" through multilevel marketing, my insecurity about the future and the allure of riches beyond my imagination left me discontent and dissatisfied with the life God had given me. And vulnerable to the devil's tactics to convince me to ease my financial burdens on my own.

God cares more about developing our character than showering us with riches. When Christ is in charge in our lives, our circumstances can transform us—whether or not our circumstances change.

MLMs appeal to our pride, greed, and discontent. If you've ever struggled with trusting God to provide to the point where you were tempted by covetousness to compromise on your beliefs, *Empty at the Top* will speak to your heart. If you've been approached by someone promoting a way to easily solve all your financial woes by taking advantage of others, read this book before taking another step in that direction. Don't go into it blind, without realizing the spiritual dangers of multilevel marketing.

PROLOGUE

When I sensed the Lord telling me He was giving me a "hard word" for the body of Christ, I wanted to do a Jonah—run. I had spent three years going in a direction opposite to what God had planned for my life. The last thing I wanted was to revisit that place of rebellion. I needed to obey and share the insights God was giving me.

I make some pretty strong statements in this book. I know I'll be stepping on some toes—because I've been there. I was once sold on the free enterprise system and the concept of creating financial independence in this lifetime. The system of building a business by selling or consuming products, and recruiting others to do the same, was for many years very dear to my heart. I turned a deaf ear to anyone with negative input or attitudes. I was trained to shut out anyone and anything that did not agree with my "success mentality." Those who were not "with us" were the enemy.

Yes, I've been where you, or someone you love, might be at this very moment. I was sold—lock, stock, and barrel—on the pursuit of the American Dream. With blinders on, I continued down a path that almost led to my spiritual destruction.

I hope my story speaks to your heart. You may not agree with my final conclusion, but I trust you'll see my heart is to see the body of Christ hungering and thirsting for more of Jesus rather than success and the things of this world.

I praise God that even when we make a mess of our lives, and finally come to the end of ourselves, He is faithful to forgive us, heal us, and deliver us.

— ***Athena Dean***

P.S. All names used in this book except for Chuck's and our children's are fictional. The stories, however, are true.

CHAPTER ONE

IT'S NOT WHAT YOU HAVE, IT'S WHAT HAS YOU

I held the envelope with its blue and gold lettering in my trembling hand. With my heart pounding in anticipation, I waved it at my husband. "How much do you think it is this month?" I asked Chuck.

He gazed up into the air as if sighting an object far out of reach. "Hmmm . . . I'll bet it's eighteen thousand dollars!"

"I think it might be more!" As I slowly pulled the check out of the envelope, I gasped at the numbers. My payment for the previous month was $21,000.00.

Chuck playfully snatched the check out of my hand. "Gimme that! I'll make a copy and keep it with the others. This really proves the dream is real!"

Now, I thought, we have enough to live the good life and share with others. We are finally cashing in on all our hard work!

Our entire family of six could now go on a week-long cruise to the Caribbean. Choosing a glitzy resort wardrobe made me feel like a movie star. We were able to buy the kids the clothes they wanted as well as extras like snowboards and skateboards for our teenage sons.

Almost completely out of debt, we had just moved into a 3,500-square-foot house with a 180-degree view of Puget Sound. For the first time in many years we had all new furniture in a brand-new house. A shiny mahogany dining room table, beveled glass in the matching china cabinet, a plush Oriental rug, and elegant maroon-and-green-striped sofas gave the upper floor an exquisite feel. Floor-to-ceiling windows framed spectacular sunsets, snowy mountain peaks, and the ever-changing gray-to-blue waters of the inland sea. The downstairs rec room where the kids could have their friends over to "hang out" was dominated by a luxury pool table with comfortable couches. It all felt so good.

But I was empty. And I didn't even know it.

Just that morning I had read Mark 8:36: "For what will it profit a man if he gains the whole world, and loses his own soul?" My eyes may have registered the words on the page, but the message had not made it to my heart. For months my devotional routine had been on automatic pilot—a quick prayer and a few minutes glancing at a Psalms. I couldn't remember the last time I heard God's voice leading me to a deeper walk with Him.

This financial dream-come-true had its beginnings a few months after Chuck and I were married in 1982. Five months before, we had been introduced to each other by my roommate Pat, a mutual friend. At the time, I was managing a successful fundraising business, and Chuck was selling services for the Church of Scientology. I saw him as a good-looking cowboy with a sense of humor and intriguing creativity. He told me I was so different from any other woman he had ever dated that his curiosity kept him coming back.

When he went clothes shopping with me in my new BMW, I ripped and tore through long racks of the finest dresses at Bonwit Teller in Beverly Hills. With a flick of my well-used credit card, I walked out with a pile of expensive dresses and suits. Chuck followed me in amazement. This was a world he had never known, but he didn't plan to leave unless I asked him to. He was having too much fun watching me!

I was never one to take the slow and steady road, whether in shopping or marriage. A few months after meeting, we took our friendship to the next level, and three months later we tied the knot on Valentine's Day.

Not long after the wedding, Chuck's friend Jason invited us to a meeting in Burbank, California. "I admire your financial success," he said in a sincere tone, "and I'd like to get your opinion on a new business venture I'm thinking about getting into. It would really help me if you'd check it out with me."

He was asking for our opinion! We felt important and flattered. Of course we could help him out!

We met Jason at a real estate office in downtown Burbank. When we walked into the darkened room, a video of an old Phil Donahue show was playing. Donahue was exposing corrupt practices in the insurance industry, which this new business was going up against. After the video ended, a down-to-earth man in his forties stood and eloquently explained the crusade. He spoke of the common-sense ideas that would help people make and save money, and sound financial principles that had been hidden from the average American family by the greedy insurance and banking industries. The "wrong" that was being perpetrated on innocent consumers quickly drew us in.

The speaker painted a picture of the deception of the corporate dream. "Do you really believe the company you work for is concerned about whether you have enough to live on when you retire? Do you think they care about you and your family?"

He expertly wove a feeling of discontentment for working nine to five for a paycheck and benefitting a large conglomerate that wouldn't be there for you when you really needed them.

"What would you do with an extra thousand or fifteen hundred dollars a month? Buy a new house, car, RV? Send your kids to private school? Travel? Retire early?" The speaker sent our minds reeling with possibilities and stirrings of dissatisfaction.

Next he explained his incredible plan. "You could start your own business and make up to two thousand dollars a month—working part time!" If we followed certain steps, and recruited friends and family, our income would increase exponentially.

The clincher came when he introduced a twenty-six-year-old guy who was making $25,000 a month after only eighteen months in the business. That convinced us. If he could do it, so could we! When he said he had only twenty kits for people to buy to get started, we scrambled to the front of the room to claim ours.

Suddenly, our fundraising business felt like a ball and chain. This opportunity seemed like something that could give us financial independence. We could work hard to build the business, then do whatever we pleased while it continued to generate income. We felt as though we were getting in on the California Gold Rush—and we wanted to sink our picks and shovels into it before anyone else!

We rushed home and shared the dream with our four young children. This could be the answer to all their dreams too. The whole family could get all the toys we'd ever wanted!

Chuck's daughter and son from a previous marriage, Roby and Ailen, were eleven and seven years old, definitely mature enough to grasp what money could buy. Although Garrett and Aaron, my two- and three-year-old boys, were too young to understand what was happening, they got excited with the rest of us.

We were so enthralled with the amazing opportunity that it didn't dawn on us that our friend Jason wasn't really looking for our opinion about joining the company. All along his plan was to recruit us. We were on his "hot list," and he used the line that he thought would get us to a meeting. It definitely worked!

The "Gold Rush"

As Chuck and I sat down eagerly with our "upline manager," he told us to make a list of at least one hundred people we knew, from friends and family to the bagger at the corner grocery store. People from school, church, PTA, relatives, the person who sold us our last car.

"When you finish listing everyone you know," the manager said, "go back and put a star next to the ones who are in some form of leadership. People who are excited, motivated, hard-working, successful, influential. These are the ones you want to recruit into your organization because they are the kind of people everyone gravitates toward."

Chuck and I are naturally outgoing, so we threw a big party at our house. That way we would have a captive audience for our first opportunity meeting. We invited two hundred prospects to hear the good news!

With the barbecue smoking in the backyard and festive music playing in the background, Jason and his upline manager helped us "work the crowd." We were convinced that we were helping our friends. After all, we had a great product that would make them money. Our zeal was boundless.

After dessert, we gathered everyone around a white board and our upline manager shared the details. People signed up like crazy. We were on our way!

The fundraising business I had established a few years earlier had been showing signs of weakening, so as fast as we could we shut that down and went full time into our new venture. With no second thoughts, we opened an office above a real estate firm in Burbank and ran newspaper ads all over town. We held two opportunity meetings a day and turned into a well-oiled dream-selling machine.

We encouraged the people we signed up with such passion and intensity, they never questioned us or our tactics.

As Chuck and I built our business, we had great training from the charismatic and motivational ex-football coach who owned the company. "If you want to do something special with your life, this is the place to do it," he told us. "We have the answer to the desperate economic situation so many families find themselves in. You have the opportunity to redirect the future of your family and friends and the generations to follow."

Being new to multilevel marketing, we modeled ourselves after the successful leaders in the company. Every month a tally of the top earners came out, and everyone's cash flow was divulged. There weren't many women on that list, which motivated me even more.

At regional and national rallies, the leader gave out T-shirts that said, "I Am Somebody," or some other motivational motto. Some people worked eighteen hours a day, seven days a week just to have their names called to go up and get a T-shirt. As someone who desperately longed for approval from a father figure, I became one of those people.

How much better could it get? We had a chance to make big money and help people at the same time. This was a crusade to right the wrongs of American big business. We were the good guys, the white hats, the knights in shining armor.

We worked night and day at a fever pitch that first year. Ailen was involved in Little League and Roby was active in drama at school. But Chuck and I were too busy chasing the dream to attend their games and performances. We clung to the idea that the results would eventually be worth the sacrifice.

We promised ourselves and the kids that this was temporary. We would build the business to the point where the momentum would self-propel, and then we could kick back and have quality time with our kids.

We weren't the only ones believing the lie.

Marina, a Mexican American with a fiery personality, quickly moved up the ladder in our company while her husband groped to find meaningful employment. Since she was so busy building her business, he took over the role of mothering their two-year-old son and three-year-old daughter. The more recognition and honor she received from her peers and the leaders, the less respect she had for her struggling husband. After they divorced, she continued to pursue success in the company, but she lost custody of her kids.

Brian and Mary spent years building their business without any real success. Brian spent so much time trying to "make it big" that Mary became bitter and resentful toward him. After many heated arguments, they divorced, breaking their seven-year-old son's heart.

Both of these couples were professing Christians.

Being Somebody

At the regional awards event, Chuck looked handsome and successful in his black tuxedo. I sat next to him in my new pink backless silk dress, my heart pounding in anticipation of hearing our names called out over the sound system. I was pretty sure we had done enough to qualify for the big promotion to regional vice president. But we had only been doing this for twelve months. No one had achieved that title in such a short time.

When the speaker said, "Chuck and Athena Dean," I smiled triumphantly and gratefully acknowledged the applause. I felt especially important and satisfied. We were well on our way to riches.

Shortly after our promotion, we moved to Washington State, where Chuck had grown up. We opened a new office there, but he soon became disinterested. The more he distanced himself from the work, the more I dove in. To Chuck, I seemed to love the pursuit more than I loved him. Feeling jealous and depressed, he communicated in ways that came across to me as critical and nagging.

I stayed away from home as often as possible so I wouldn't have to hear his griping. Several times we reached the brink of divorce. Each time I gave him an ultimatum: "Either you accept me the way I am or I'll leave." He'd stifle his dissatisfaction and we stayed together. Chuck put up with my workaholism and drive for recognition just to keep our marriage together.

Even though we were bringing in $50,000 a year, overhead was so high that we were perpetually broke. I somehow managed to generate barely enough cash to cover the office rent, long-distance bills, advertising expenses, and travel and entertainment.

When we hit the coveted $100,000 mark, our expenses far exceeded our income. But the need to look successful resulted in huge payments on cars, offices, furniture, and our home. While everything on the outside looked great, our marriage was on the edge of disaster, and the stress of our financial situation added fuel to the fire.

I had become a prisoner of my own lustful heart. While I thought I was proving my success by the things I owned, those things actually owned me. I was miserable. Since I had never learned to value relationships, my dreams for my marriage, family, and personal life revolved around having possessions, not about anything of lasting value.

QUESTIONS FOR PERSONAL REFLECTION OR
Small Group Study

---

1. "The last thing I wanted was to revisit that place of rebellion." In your financial, marital, or spiritual situation, is there something God is telling you that you don't want to hear? Where is your "place of rebellion?"

2. Let's talk about your dream: Can you describe it? Honestly, what do you really want in life? Psychologists and sociologists tell us we all want "security" and "significance." How does your dream encompass these?

3. Mark 8:36: "For what will it profit a man if he gains the whole world, and loses his own soul?" Is it possible to pursue your dream and not lose your soul? What is involved in pursuing a dream that makes it a danger to your soul?

4. "We clung to the idea that the results would eventually be worth the sacrifice." How about you? What sacrifices are you making for the dream? Are they going to eventually prove worth it?

CHAPTER TWO

LOOKING FOR LOVE IN ALL THE WRONG PLACES

I've been told I'm a capable person, someone who gets things accomplished. Through experience I've found that God has gifted me with the ability to organize, inspire, and lead large groups of people toward a stated goal. Part of my gift is the ability to learn quickly any new technique or lesson. Picking up on things and doing them well right off the bat isn't difficult for me.

My shakier character traits center around my inability to get close to people and allow them to get close to me. Because of this shortcoming, I tend to put more importance on projects than on people, with more desire for business success than for strong relationships. I can also be very self-centered. It's a real struggle for me to think of the needs of other people before I think about myself.

I'm like my father in many ways. He was a workaholic who put his entire life into financial success, never devoting much time or effort to the relationships he had with those who loved him. Like my dad, I'm also an excitable person and smile a lot. If I like something, I say so, and others get excited in the process.

There's certainly nothing wrong with the gifts God gave me, as long as they don't get used in the wrong way. For a long time, I believed that business was where I was supposed to use my abilities.

A God-Shaped Hole

When I was nine years old, my family often visited my cousins in Alabama, and on Sundays we went with them to the Catholic church. In the towering sanctuary, I felt a quiet reverence for God that I had never experienced anywhere else. I sensed something holy there, the awesome presence of the God of the universe. Being in a place where people desired to surrender their lives to God was a new experience for me. During those times, I longed to know what God had in mind for me. One time I even thought about what it might be like to become a nun.

I got along pretty well with my peers, but I invariably tried to win the games we played—and usually did. I had to make sure everyone knew I was a winner! I'm sure that got old after a while.

As a teen, my longing for spiritual things was replaced with a desire to get attention from boys. I also fell in love with horses. The chance to compete in equestrian shows intrigued me. I poured my life into striving to be the one in the middle of the ring receiving a blue ribbon for winning the championship. Competing in big-time horse shows became an all-consuming passion for me.

My mom came to every horse show and practice session I had. But she was a perfectionist and wanted me to do everything exactly right. She meant well, but her frequent criticism communicated rejection to my young heart.

I rarely seemed to measure up to my "perfect" big brother. Jim was quiet and cooperative, an A student, and he liked all the activities Mom did—classical music, opera, and intellectual pursuits. I, on the other hand, was a strong-willed child, always pushing my mother to the limits of her patience. I never dressed the way she liked or followed the rules of etiquette at the dinner table.

My dad, on the other hand, was very nurturing—when he was around. He sang old commercial jingles to me and gave me over-the-top compliments. "Athena, if there was a field with a thousand young ladies in it, and if I was flying over in my helicopter, I would look over the other lassies and pick you out, because you are so special." He made me feel important. But because he was such a workaholic, those times of nurturing were few and far between.

I knew my father worked long hours to give me the opportunity to succeed in competitive riding, which was important to me. But I sometimes wondered, if I wasn't number one, would Dad still love me? The question haunted me.

I vied for his attention by winning the blue ribbon in every horse show I could. The fear of being rejected by my father burned deep within me. It fueled the ambitious thrust that would become a dominant factor in my actions and decisions the rest of my life.

I was raised to be self-sufficient and to fill that God-shaped hole with anything but Jesus.

Trying Hard Not to Get Saved

Chuck and I had been married for four years when the final straw hit. At thirty-three years of age, I was making big money in insurance and securities, ranking in the top 2 percent of the company's salespeople. Meanwhile, Chuck got fanatically involved in an organization that protested paying taxes and radically opposed the government structure of the United States. When the IRS and state's attorney general came after Chuck for his questionable practices of using a "warehouse bank" to turn his federal reserve notes into gold and silver without reporting it to the IRS, my business was threatened.

Chuck ranted, "I don't see how you can sell people those so-called investments when they aren't even backed by real money!"

I raged back, "Get real, Chuck! You can't just drop out of the system!"

I made up my mind. The relationship was over.

A few dozen of the people in my downline were gathering at a Christian retreat center in the mountains to spend the weekend sharing dreams, bonding, setting goals, and encouraging one another. I decided to join them, mostly to avoid Chuck, who had become a sniveling wreck, crying and begging me to change my mind about divorcing him.

I didn't really pay much attention to the speakers at the retreat. That weekend, I was surrounded by Christians, so I made a point of biting my tongue when they talked about Jesus.

When I returned home, Chuck had undergone a complete change. He seemed peaceful, calm, serene. He no longer whined and felt sorry for himself.

I couldn't put my finger on what had gotten into him, but I didn't feel as anxious for him to leave.

One of my business associates told me Chuck had accepted Jesus into his heart while I was at the retreat. I was floored. *Chuck, a Christian? No way!* That was against everything we ever stood for. We'd always thought of Christians as wimps. After all, when you're as talented and capable as we were, who needed a crutch like Jesus?

Over the years we had been in and out of Unity, Scientology, meditation, astrology, channeling—but Christianity? Our involvement in the new age practices felt safe. Each so-called religion taught that man was basically good and that we could determine our own destiny. Christianity communicated that people are weaklings who needed a Savior.

Chuck getting saved felt to me like he was going backward. But I didn't let it bother me too much because I was still divorcing him.

Over the next three days, I continued to witness incredible changes in my husband. He was soft, tender, loving, and gentle, yet also strong, confident, and courageous.

I didn't know what to think about that. But I began to feel dissatisfied with myself. Something grated inside me every time I took the Lord's name in vain. I even began to wonder if I'd made a mistake by insisting on the divorce.

When Chuck sheepishly asked, "Could we just give it one more go?" I said, "Okay, I guess you don't have to leave." I felt as if someone else spoke the words. My inner voice chided me. *How could you have said that?*

His face beamed. "Oh, Athena, I knew God would heal our marriage! Thank You, Jesus!"

Now I faced a dilemma. If we were going to stay together, I probably needed to become one of those Christians too. But what would I tell all the people who'd heard me say that Christians were wimps? I didn't want to be seen as weak.

Five weeks after Chuck got saved, my upline in the financial services business, also a Christian, called to say he was coming into town in a few weeks. I asked Monty if he could help me understand what had happened to my husband, and he sent me a copy of *Mere Christianity*, telling me we could talk when he arrived. I made it about halfway through the book when tears began coursing down my cheeks. I knew I needed to give my heart to Jesus, as outlandish as it sounded.

By the time Monty arrived I was nearly frantic. "I need to say that prayer to get saved. But I don't know how to do it. Would you help me?"

He led me in the sinner's prayer. As I prayed, I felt overwhelming relief, knowing I'd been forgiven for all the rebellion and sin littering the thirty-three years I'd lived on earth. I felt like a new person—washed clean. The load of guilt that had weighed me down and made me bitter and hard was gone, even though it would take me years to learn the depths of God's love for me. I felt like my heart of stone had been replaced with a heart of flesh.

My Kingdom Come!

I had no foundation or knowledge of Scripture. But Chuck's father was a pastor, so he had a tremendous amount of biblical knowledge imbedded into him as a child, and it all came flooding back to him. He fully grasped the elements of faith and the importance of renewing his thought patterns with promises and truths of God.

We were worlds apart, even after we were both saved. Chuck surrendered completely to Jesus, but I stood firm in my pride.

Deep down I knew if I really surrendered to Jesus, He would ask me to give up my drive for wealth and recognition. I wasn't ready for that. I wanted *my kingdom* to come and *my will* to be done. I was glad to be on my way to heaven, but I couldn't relinquish my world of competition, success, and recognition. I prayed and attended church, yet I still longed for the things of this world.

The people I was involved with in my business had become my family. They gave me the strokes that affirmed and flattered me. They never asked me how my relationships with my children were going or what my real motives were for working so hard. My entire social life revolved around work. If a person didn't help me financially, I didn't waste my time building a relationship with him or her.

Since I'd already caused enough damage to my kids from neglect, I kept my time with them at a minimum. It was easier to stay away from them so I wouldn't have to confront the pain I had caused them.

While Chuck and I now had Jesus in common, we had completely different missions in life. I still spent every waking hour thinking about the business. All he cared about was telling people about Jesus.

One day Chuck came home from Bible school, where he had been reading a book by Oswald Chambers titled *So Send I You*, and said, "We're going to Africa!"

"Excuse me?"

"Or maybe Asia or Russia, I don't care. I just know we're supposed to go preach the gospel to the nations!" Chuck's intensity almost knocked me over.

"That's great, dear," I responded sourly. "I hope you have a good time."

QUESTIONS FOR PERSONAL REFLECTION OR *Small Group Study*

1. "Through experience I've found that God has gifted me with the ability to organize, inspire, and lead large groups of people toward a stated goal." What gifts do you possess that make you a good leader? Does your giftedness have anything to do with how you are seeking to fulfill your dream?

2. "I tend to put more importance on projects than on people." Does this describe you? Be honest, do you feel yourself drawn more to embracing the project than people? Describe an instance that demonstrates your answer.

3. "She meant well, but her frequent criticism communicated rejection to my young heart." "He made me feel important" From whom have you been rejected in your life? In contrast, who has accepted you? How did that effect decisions you have made or the trajectory of your life?

4. "I couldn't put my finger on what had gotten into him; Chuck surrendered completely to Jesus, but I stood firm in my pride." How would others describe your spiritual life? Does God's love show in the things you cherish and strive for?

5. "While Chuck and I now had Jesus in common, we had completely different missions in life." How does fulfilling your "dream" fit with completing God's mission in your life?

CHAPTER THREE

IT ALL SOUNDED SO GOOD!

By spending seventy hours a week becoming an expert in my financial services business, I felt I was on my way to becoming an expert on network marketing. I wrote books about how to succeed in that arena. I woke up at 6:00 every morning with my wheels turning, a rush of adrenaline surging through me as I anticipated what the day would hold. From that first cup of coffee to the last satisfied look at my DayTimer in the evening, I was completely focused.

As I gleaned the inner workings of multilevel marketing (MLM for short), I realized that it combines two proven concepts in the world of business: networking and marketing. Marketing is the practice of moving goods and services through distribution channels from manufacturer to consumer. Networking is the joining of people who share resources and knowledge to accomplish common goals.

In an MLM business, you develop a structure of salespeople by recruiting them into your organization, called a downline.

Through those individuals, the company's products or services are sold. Sometimes the distributor is the consumer. Or the distributor sells the product or service to the consumer. Either way, without the distributor buying for personal use or selling to make a profit, the company doesn't make any money.

Rather than spending a predetermined amount on advertising, the company pays the distributors to advertise their product by word of mouth. Distributors make their money from personal sales, bonuses, and commissions on the sales volume of the distributors in their downline.

Most companies have figured out that multilevel marketing has developed a bad reputation, so they go to great lengths to try to make their distribution system sound like something else. They call it by different names, such as network marketing, direct selling, direct marketing, direct sales.

They have also become cunning with the ways they distance themselves from words that link them to the network marketing business model. Instead of distributors or independent agents, recruits are now called advisors, health coaches, financial agents, business leaders, executive coaches, wealth consultants, and other important-sounding titles.

I recently met a woman who was involved in a home party plan that sold jewelry. She was offended when I called her company a multilevel marketer, adamantly insisting it was not. She had more than twenty people under her and was encouraged to build a larger downline so she could make overrides on others and not have to work so hard herself.

If you have to recruit distributors in order to make the big money, it's definitely some form of multilevel marketing, no matter what name it is called.

Cruising for Christians

"Just think, Chuck," I mused out loud, "if I can make it to senior vice president, I'll qualify for an extra ten thousand dollars a month. If I get other believers involved, we could all make our dreams come true for the Lord."

Chuck agreed that there was plenty we could do with that much extra money. But he wasn't much interested in helping me do it.

Chuck enrolled in Cascade Bible College in Bellevue, Washington. While there he heard about Point Man Ministries, a Christian outreach for Vietnam veterans by Vietnam veterans. After praying, he felt that this was where the Lord wanted him to serve.

When the ministry's founder died, his widow asked Chuck to take over the ministry. He spent all his time creating a network of Christian Vietnam veterans to help those vets who still hadn't been healed spiritually. He found other born-again Vietnam veterans who had a burden to share about their relationships with Jesus with other hopeless and hurting vets.

It all sounded so good! I would recruit other Christians into my business and make a ton of money so my husband could be supported in full-time ministry. Perfect! "Just imagine all the vets we could get saved in the places we could travel to reach them!"

I used the good motivation of funding the ministry to justify my lust for more money. I convinced myself I was doing a good thing for people. After all, with more income, I could donate to missions and help Christians get out of debt. But in my heart, I was far from seeking God's will for my life.

Who Do You Know?

I easily used my relationships with influential people in the church to advance my business. My standard pitch went something like this: "John, I know how busy you are with your ministry, but who do you know who might be interested in earning an extra five hundred to a thousand dollars a month working part time?" I asked if they could help me out by referring me to others. Since people who supported their ministries would feel compelled to support them, it would be easy for them to create a lucrative endeavor.

With the extra money, I figured I could fund the printing and distribution of *Reveille*, Point Man's free newspaper for vets. I could help underwrite the new building project at church and support foreign missionaries.

But when the cash came in, greed followed. Moving to a nicer house, trading in my car for a more expensive model, taking the family on a cruise, buying a new wardrobe, and having extra spending money crowded out the godly things I planned.

I was so busy working, I never really listened for God's voice. I just did whatever I thought sounded good and then asked God to bless it. I wanted to build a big business for the recognition I would receive more than I wanted to glorify God.

I ignored 1 John 2:15–16, which says, "Do not love the world or the things in the world. If anyone loves the world, the love of the Father is not in him. For all that is in the world—the lust of the flesh, the lust of the eyes, and the pride of life—is not of the Father but is of the world."

I'm not the only one who has fallen into this deception. Countless sincere Christians in the American church have succumbed to the allure of multilevel marketing schemes. MLMs love to target stay-at-home moms, luring them with the opportunity to make extra income to add to the family coffers. Many of these women are Jesus followers who take their mothering seriously by not working outside the home. MLM infiltrates Christian homes and sucks the true life out of them.

Almost every organization that manufactures consumer items encourages its salespeople to utilize their personal relationships to build their business. Whether it's real estate, insurance, automobiles, weight loss, cosmetics, vitamins, or privately owned retail establishments, those who represent their products or services often look for prospects at their place of worship.

Christians naturally network at church, exchanging business cards with other parishioners and "working the crowd." Before long they become so successful they hardly have time to go to church. When they do, it's not to get fed and grow in the things of God, it's to conduct business.

By bringing our (so-called) opportunity into the church, we have become like the money changers in the temple. Jesus did not take what these men were doing lightly. He said, "Take these things away! Do not make My Father's house a house of merchandise!" (John 2:16). Oh, how we defile the house of God by bringing our business with us to church!

QUESTIONS FOR PERSONAL REFLECTION OR
Small Group Study

1. "From that first cup of coffee to the last satisfied look at my Day Timer in the evening, I was completely focused." What fills your calendar? When you discover what fills your time you will be able to clearly articulate your priorities. Discuss what occupies your days.

2. "I was so busy working, I never really listened for God's voice. I just did whatever I thought sounded good and then asked God to bless it." How can you be fully aware of God's voice in the decisions you make in your business?

3. 1 John 2:15–16 says, "Do not love the world or the things in the world. If anyone loves the world, the love of the Father is not in him. For all that is in the world—the lust of the flesh, the lust of the eyes, and the pride of life—is not of the Father but is of the world." How does this verse relate to your business? Is there a part of your dream that fits that description?

4. "Take these things away! Do not make My Father's house a house of merchandise!" (John 2:16). Have you seen people "selling" something at your church? Describe how that made you feel.

CHAPTER FOUR

GOD'S IDEA OR GOOD IDEA?

*E*ighteen months after I'd been saved, I was making over $100,000 a year and still wasn't satisfied. Chuck and I considered moving back to California, because all the top earners who'd stayed there when we moved to Washington were now making twice the income I was. I prayed every day, "Your will, not mine, Lord. Have Your way. Change my heart to desire Your will."

Chuck was willing to put Point Man on hold to help me build my business so it could fund the ministry the way we wanted.

One Sunday evening, Chuck spoke at a service at our church. In the year and a half that we had been saved, this was the first time I was going to hear him talk about how God had reached his soul. I'd been so busy doing my thing I didn't know what was happening in my husband's life.

As I sat in the back row and listened, I saw his heart and began to see how God was using him. I wept.

I sensed the Lord speaking quietly to the depths of my spirit. *Walk away from the business and help Chuck in the ministry.*

The words were clearly from the Lord. But immediately fear set in. I tried to convince myself the voice I'd heard was not God's.

After the service, a lady approached me. She didn't have a clue about our situation or plans. But she said to me, "Don't be surprised if your plans change."

That really was God speaking to me! I needed to make a choice to soften my heart. However at that point the ministry income was only about $500 a month. How was a family of six going to exist on that?

Fully realizing the message was from God meant I didn't need to worry. He was changing my heart to desire His will, and He was having His way—just as I had prayed.

God's Way of Doing Business

Once I started to make the transition and turn my business over to my upline director, I had many thoughts about how I could help expand the ministry. Surely there had to be grant money available for an organization that was helping Vietnam veterans. I could increase the donor base by mailing out letters to raise support.

As I submitted what I thought were great ideas to the Lord, He made it clear He had another plan in mind.

Pray. That was all He said to me.

Sure, God, I'll pray. But I've got to do *something, don't I?*

No.

God wanted to prove to me that He is my provider. If I brought in the money by great fundraising programs, how would I ever know if it was God or me making it happen? I had to learn to trust Him, and that meant staying out of the process so He could provide.

There were times when we had to get our meals from the food bank. But God was always faithful.

One Friday morning we received a disconnect notice for nonpayment of the ministry phone bill. If we didn't pay $400 by Monday at 5:00 p.m., they would turn off the phones. I asked for an extension but was denied. We had no money in the bank. Most of our donations came through the mail, and there would be no mail on Monday because it was a holiday. This was the end of the line.

Desperate for an answer from God, I went to a retreat center where I could fast and pray. I was sure God was trying to say something to me. But what? Had I committed some awful sin? Mishandled the finances of the ministry?

As I confessed everything I could think of, God brought to mind my habit of being disrespectful in my marriage. I sometimes made fun of Chuck just to get a laugh. My sarcastic attitude grieved the Holy Spirit.

After I repented for my wrong attitude toward my husband, I felt a spiritual release and went home.

On Sunday afternoon, Marc, a Vietnam vet we ministered to occasionally, came to our home. "I don't know why," he said, "but the Lord told me to empty out my savings account and give you this money." Though Marc often struggled with unemployment, he handed Chuck and me four hundred dollars. The exact amount we needed to pay the phone bill!

God has met our needs over and over in many creative ways. It never ceases to amaze us the way He orchestrates circumstances to help our faith grow. He has always been faithful to provide for our family.

The next five years were filled with adventures in faith as we followed His lead in the ministry.

Still, there were areas of my heart I had not completely yielded to the Lord.

Setting a Bad Example

Being a type-A personality, I threw myself into ministry work with the same intensity I put into my business. Soon it became as much of an idol to me as striving for financial success had. I never slowed down long enough to let the Lord heal areas in my life that were causing my dysfunctional behavior. So I set an unhealthy and damaging example for others in the ministry.

Chuck and I worked six days a week, sometimes seven, for five years without ever taking a break. Most Sundays we spoke in churches. We rarely spent time with our children.

We wanted to always be available to help those who were hurting. The demands in the veteran community were so great that we often found ourselves ministering over the phone after work hours. This schedule took its toll on us, and burnout set in. Daniel 7:25 says "And shall wear out the saints of the most High" (KJV). It definitely is a strategy of the enemy of our soul to keep us so busy chasing success. I allowed people and circumstances to wear me down to the point where I was operating in the flesh.

As I spoke at conferences about healing from posttraumatic stress disorder, I discovered that PTSD didn't only apply to veterans. Anyone who has experienced severe wounding is susceptible. The symptoms include depression, rage, isolation, difficulty with close personal relationships, suicidal tendencies, and substance abuse.

Many wives of Vietnam veterans, including Christians, suffer with PTSD from childhood sexual abuse, growing up in alcoholic families, traumas such as abortion, rape, and domestic violence.

Having been a battered wife from my previous marriage, I had a burden to work with women who needed healing. It seemed evident that God was calling me to a ministry of restoration among Christian women. So I stepped down from my administrative duties at Point Man.

One morning in July of 1991, during the Point Man annual campout, as I was journaling my prayers, I sensed the Lord telling me His will for me was to be still and discover how to clearly discern the whispers of God. If I listened to the Holy Spirit above all others, including myself, I would never be led astray. Then He could say, "This is the way, walk in it" (Isaiah 30:21), and by following His direction, I would be able to stay on track. I'd know the difference between a "good idea" and God's idea.

Back in Disobedience

At church one month later, a woman told me she felt led to give me a bottle of herbs to help me lose weight without diet or exercise. She said if I liked them and wanted to sell the product, she'd help me. Since I was in the ministry, she offered to pay for me to sign up as a distributor.

I tried the herbs, and my mind began racing and my body nearly burst with energy. I did some research and discovered the product was made up of four herbs, one of which was a natural form of the drug known as speed. Even though several medical sources warned against taking that herb, it caused such an enthralling feeling that I didn't want to believe it could be dangerous. Besides, the naturopathic doctor who developed the concoction, and leaders in the multilevel organization that was marketing the product, offered numerous reassurances. I chose to listen to the sources who didn't give warnings.

I felt so good I didn't bother praying about it. The idea of just sitting at the feet of Jesus had lost its appeal. I didn't ask God if I should get involved. It seemed right, so I went for it. After five years in the ministry with limited funds and denying myself luxuries, I was ready to make some money again. My direction from the Lord to listen to His voice became a distant memory.

In August of 1992, a year after I jumped back into the business world, Chuck called me from the Point Man office and said, "Athena, I'm not coming home until you make an about-face. You're not here for me like I need you to be, and I can't handle it anymore."

His threat got my attention . . . for a little while. But soon things went back to normal.

Finally, in desperation, Chuck delegated his responsibilities to some of the other leaders and walked away from his calling to Vietnam veterans. He could have continued with my administrative help. But I was too busy doing my thing to notice he needed me. Once I got back on the MLM roller coaster, I stopped encouraging him and nurturing him in his ministry and in our marriage. I became self-centered to the point of being blind to the needs of my husband and family.

QUESTIONS FOR PERSONAL REFLECTION OR
Small Group Study

---

1. "God's Idea or Good Idea?" Is the primary drive of your life God's idea or just a good idea? Could you convince a jury of your peers of your answer? Articulate it here.

2. "The words were clearly from the Lord. But immediately fear set in. I tried to convince myself the voice I'd heard was not God's." Have you ever sensed God telling you something? Was your response to listen or to ignore? Think about it, then describe the argument between you and God.

3. "But she said to me, 'Don't be surprised if your plans change.'" Has God ever changed your plans? Are you brave enough to talk about it? Share your experience.

4. "Soon [serving in ministry] became as much of an idol to me as striving for financial success had. I never slowed down long enough to let the Lord heal areas in my life that were causing my dysfunctional behavior." Have you experienced a dysfunctional behavior in serving God? Has serving God ever become an idol? What happened to bring awareness to the surface?

CHAPTER FIVE

DOING THE WRONG THING FOR THE RIGHT REASON

My moneymaking days seemed a lifetime ago, but I quickly reverted to that mentality. Ideas flowed for selling the herbs and I eagerly anticipated all the money I could make. I knew what it was like to be on the receiving end of charity. The tables were turned. Now I could be the one to sow into those who gave their lives for the gospel.

Quiet times with the Lord were far from my mind.

I started losing weight so fast it seemed too good to be true. Little did I know that using those herbs over a long period of time could damage my adrenal glands and endocrine system.

Credibility at Work

To build my team with this new product, I ran ads on a Christian radio station. Chuck and I had been interviewed many times on

Seattle-area stations as well as the 700 Club and other national shows. I figured that my credibility in ministry would attract honest, hard-working Christians onto my team. I believed the company I represented had a great product and offered a wonderful opportunity. This opportunity would allow Christians to get out of debt, send their children to private schools, and fund ministry projects or missionaries.

Several wonderful people replied to my ads, and many got started with me in my new business. Some had sales and MLM background, others did not.

Three months later, I got a call from my upline director. "Have you heard? The doctor who allegedly discovered the herbal formula apparently ripped it off from the manufacturer! Half the company is leaving to start another company."

A large group of distributors made serious accusations against the leaders of the company. After criticizing the management team, they quit to join companies with copycat products.

By this time my income was up to $10,000 per month. I deafened my ears to the scores of negatives, protected my group against the "gossip," and defended the founder and the company's reputation. For three months we did not get paid, but I believed what I wanted to be the truth.

Since I was one of the top producers, I received preferential treatment. I received my pay two of those three months, so it was easy for me to look past the negatives. In my mind, the crisis was due to "the enemy" trying to destroy what God was doing in my life.

When allegations cropped up that the founder was involved in new age practices, and on his fourth marriage, I still chose to look the other way. I thought I could influence the company leadership and not be affected myself.

The Money Rolls In

By the end of my first year with the herb company, we had weathered three major management turnovers and numerous months when no one got paid. Many people left the organization, but I was determined to help save the company. After all, I had a vested interest. I had earned over $100,000 that first year.

In January of 1993, I began a mega-blitz of ads on local Christian radio stations as well as many across the country. Within four months, my income went from $10,000 to $19,000 a month. It continued to climb by $2-3,000 every month. Others in my downline were seeing their income doubling and tripling. We felt our persistence and loyalty was paying off.

Then Chuck and I came up with a grand plan. Why not cash in on this big downline and open a product distribution center for the company? One of our directors offered to put up some of the money as a sort of financing. That led to the notion of creating a corporation and selling stock to select Christian directors in my downline. Clearly this was the perfect way to fund our training center and make a percentage on the purchases that were already being made by my organization.

I jumped wholeheartedly into the challenge of the venture. But Chuck began to have second thoughts.

"This fiasco is going to eat up even more of your time, Athena." He pleaded with me to drop it, but we were too far into the planning process for me to rescind my support. With plans in motion and my adrenaline flowing, that was the last thing I wanted to do.

I disobeyed my husband, and he let me get away with it.

A group of twelve of us met and shared plans for how we could make it happen. We built many benefits for shareholders into the agreement. With the growth rate we were experiencing, we felt it would only be a short time before we would all see an incredible profit. A distribution center would make it easier for us to build our personal downlines.

I excitedly spent all my time setting up shop in our leased office space. I had a sales counter built, bought furniture, fixtures, and signs, and designed four-color sales aids.

The first month we brought in over $100,000 in business, and the second month we did $175,000. Everyone was proud and happy. Good relationships were built among the shareholders, who took turns manning the office.

When one of the leaders in our company wanted to buy distribution rights to part of the territory in our county, greed kicked in and I moved to buy it for the shareholders. I felt we should have the territory rather than this unscrupulous Mormon businessman. To swing the purchase of new territory, the shareholders brought in nine additional people from their downlines, all of whom were Christians.

While we were still experiencing growth, we noticed troubling signals from the home office. They made changes that directly affected our sales.

After a local newspaper published an exposé on the herbal product we were selling, our business slipped into uncertainty. The bad press unsettled our loyal follower base. Confidence in the product eroded. We tried to rally the troops by refuting the allegations at meetings, where we trained them on the "hidden agenda" of the newspaper and the governmental agency involved. We made a good case, but we still lost a lot of business.

We continued to operate as if the money was still pouring in. But our monthly sales dropped significantly over the next few months.

Not wanting to face what was happening, the board of directors and I kept hiring office workers to keep up with the paperwork the home office required. Rather than consult the board, I made decisions on my own and let them know afterward, figuring it was easier and faster to get things done that way. I didn't realize I was negating my protective covering, leaving myself wide open for attack from the board.

In October, at the company's annual convention, I put all my troubling thoughts away for the evening, anticipating the award I was about to receive. I was the first person who would be honored with the esteemed Ambassador Star Director position. In the elegant hotel banquet room, wearing a rich purple dress with sequins, I walked from table to table greeting everyone and basking in the power and prestige. Two thirds of those attending the convention were in my sales organization. Almost all the men and women going up to the stage to win prizes and be recognized were on my team.

While we were all Christians and gave the Lord credit for our success, there was still a lot of pride, arrogance, and flesh in control. We felt superior to the other teams in the company because we were so righteous and honest.

That night, the spotlight was on income, worldly success, and recognition. My team and I all graciously received the awards we were expecting, thanking God in our acceptance speeches.

The very next month the company made a major change in the compensation plan, which decreased the pay of our workers by 50 percent.

I felt a tiny tug of fear. Had I been in denial about this company? My stomach felt like lead as I called the home office. In response to my questions, I got double-talk. The people I trusted and had defended failed me.

How could I go on promoting the integrity of this company? I felt betrayed and used. Still, I frantically sought a way to make it work.

In the months that followed it became clear to me that I had made a terrible mistake. Because of my endorsement, many Christians had committed to representing a company that had unethical leadership and products that were not entirely safe.

Finally seeing I had no future with this organization, I started looking for different opportunities to represent. Uppermost in my thoughts was having additional options to offer my downline.

As I vocalized my disappointment with the leadership, dissention rose up in our co-op. Some were still loyal to the business and blamed me for the financial problems. Others supported me.

Putting a Band-Aid on a Bullet Hole

To try to keep the ball rolling, I rushed into another business. A friend who was in full-time ministry sent me information on a large Canadian conglomerate that had recently launched its product line in the US using multilevel marketing as their distribution method. This organization dealt in communications products with a hefty price tag. The video presentation sold me on their excellent product, sound financial management, and the corporation's integrity.

I quickly got the team together to take a look at this exciting opportunity. It appeared to be a legitimate alternative, and the potential for making money seemed good. So I didn't really pray about it.

I spent six months trying to rebuild my reputation and track record, filling the need in my heart for recognition and importance.

But this move created more disunity among the shareholders, and rumors began to fly. The herbal product enterprise terminated my contract for getting involved with another organization. I resigned from the board of directors so the co-op could continue to provide product to local distributors. But to those who had stayed loyal to the firm, I became the enemy. My friends turned against me. I felt defensive, anxious, and uncertain. I hated feeling out of control.

When the co-op received confirmation about documented cases of people getting sick on the product, they demanded a recall of particular lot numbers. The leadership team refused to take responsibility.

At the same time, we discovered the consultants running the company dropped its liability insurance that covered distributors. That was the last straw.

With what I felt was righteous indignation, I decided I could no longer keep selling the product to distributors. I notified the shareholders of my intention to sell all assets and cash them all out. Everyone took an enormous hit. I felt responsible, and I was determined to make it right somehow.

My most devastating loss was the deterioration of this group of believers. Friends started bickering and soon became enemies. People who used to drop in daily for fellowship now steered clear of me. Conversations that used to be filled with joy, prayer, and love were now chillingly polite. We had come together as Christians, but our overriding motive was the desire to make money. When the money was gone, many of the relationships disappeared.

QUESTIONS FOR PERSONAL REFLECTION OR
Small Group Study

1. "Doing the Wrong Thing for the Right Reason" Have you found yourself acting out this statement? Tell about your experience.

2. "I still chose to look the other way." What have you seen that you chose to ignore? Talk about it along with the outcome.

3. "While we were all Christians and gave the Lord credit for our success, there was still a lot of pride, arrogance, and flesh in control." Even ministry can be done in pride and arrogance. Describe what you've experienced in the Christian arena that looked much like the world.

4. "My friends turned against me. I felt defensive, anxious, and uncertain. I hated feeling out of control." Have you ever had those you trusted turn against you? How did that make you feel? Sometimes people betray us, sometimes we betray them. Tell of your experiences, and how they affected the direction of your life.

5. "We had come together as Christians, but our overriding motive was the desire to make money. When the money was gone, many of the relationships disappeared." Have you ever experienced a situation like this? What was the result? Read Luke 15:11-32. What was the response of the son who lost everything? What encouragement does this parable offer to this circumstance?

CHAPTER SIX

FATAL ATTRACTIONS

In my drive for financial success, I naturally grew further and further apart from my husband. While Chuck was involved in ministry, I was a lone ranger in running our company. Chuck cared about people getting saved, concerned about where they would spend eternity. I cared about getting people involved in the organization, wanting to help them make money, which would result in more money for me. In conversations, Chuck focused on glorifying God. I focused on the exciting venture I was part of.

Because I was out of the biblical order for husband-and-wife relationships, I was no longer under the protection of the spiritual head of our household. I did whatever I wanted, whenever I wanted, without consulting Chuck. This left me wide open to error because I was ignoring the spiritual covering God had placed in my life.

I was too busy for prayer and Bible study in the mornings. Any prayer I managed to cram in was just a lengthy list of wants and needs along with thanksgiving for financial blessings. I never stopped to quiet my soul to listen to God's voice and receive His instruction for the day. I certainly did not spend the time necessary with the Lord to allow Him to convict me when I was in error.

Because of my lack of Christian disciplines, I became susceptible to ungodly suggestions. Enticed by flattery and driven by my desire for recognition based on what I could accomplish, I was a prime target for the enemy.

The temptations of power, sex, and money have derailed the fruitful ministries of numerous pastors and Christian leaders. Many of these are men. Could it be that multilevel marketing and similar systems attract women who long for someone to make them feel good about themselves?

Melanie was so motivated by sales contests that she worked long hours, depriving herself of sleep, just to be recognized as a winner. She grew up with alcoholic parents and never received the love or nurturing she so desperately needed as a child.

When men who are paid to "motivate the troops" compliment vulnerable women and encourage them in their businesses, unhealthy attraction easily kicks in. Many women, single and married, fall for men with whom they are involved in business. With so much in common and extended hours spent together, they form bonds that can become inappropriate.

My friend Marnie, who was on my team, had a strong walk with the Lord. She discipled me when I was beginning to learn how to surrender to Jesus. Her marriage went through hard times when her husband served time in prison. But even while they were separated, their relationship remained strong because they both loved the Lord.

I introduced Marnie and others on my team to some of the "big boys" who ran the company. One of them, Nathan, a professing Christian, was a smooth-talking, motivational, dynamic, good-looking man from the South. He watched out for my interests and made sure my team and I received preferential treatment. He spent a lot of time "selling the dream" to us. We'd all go out for dessert after the evening meetings, and we'd talk, laugh, cry, and dream together for hours into the night.

Marnie and Nathan began spending time alone together. After a while, she quit visiting her husband in prison. And that was the end of her marriage.

I was indignant that she allowed herself to fall for the ambush the enemy had set. Surely she was stronger and wiser than that! First Corinthians 10:12 says, "Let him who thinks he stands take heed lest he fall."

I criticized my friend for her lack of discernment. But a month later, I got sucked into the same trap.

Chuck was out of town a lot, speaking to veterans' groups. I traveled frequently for my business. On one trip, one of the company's new bigwigs began to play me. Perry called me two or three times a day to see how he could help me with my organization. He always asked about my personal life. I'm sure his motivation was to strengthen my devotion to the company so my sales volume would continue to grow. But he made me feel important and needed.

When he crossed the line from business to flirting, I didn't even notice.

One night, as Perry and I sat across from each other in the restaurant of our conference hotel, relaxing after a big meeting, Perry said, "Athena, you did a great job tonight. If it weren't for your leadership, I don't know what we would do." He winked at me and said, "And you sure have nice eyes."

After that I became preoccupied with thoughts about how I could impress Perry with my wit, talents, and looks. I made sure I was at any meeting he attended and we orchestrated our schedules so he would be wherever I was teaching. By God's grace, I did not commit physical adultery. But as Matthew 5:28 points out, if you've lusted in your mind, you're just as guilty.

Chuck sensed I was drifting away and finally confronted me. "Athena, things haven't been right between us, and you know it. You've never been able to keep secrets from me. So what's going on?"

With tears, I confessed my sin. And begged him to help me.

Chuck and I retraced the steps leading to my deception. We spent three months going over the subtle choices I'd made that took me down the wrong path so I'd be able to foresee my areas of vulnerability in the future.

I realized that as soon as I quit praying every day, getting into the Word, spending quality quiet time at Jesus's feet, and listening for His voice, my ability to discern good from evil crashed.

I praise God I had a husband who was understanding enough to help me set boundaries and who loved me enough to forgive.

Focusing on success can be dangerous for a Christian. We can become so consumed that our devotion to Jesus takes second place. When that happens, making wrong choices is inevitable.

I was not in the Word enough to pay attention to the warnings of 1 Timothy 6:6–11 (NIV):

> Godliness with contentment is great gain. For we brought nothing into the world, and we can take nothing out of it. But if we have food and clothing, we will be content with that. Those who want to get rich fall into temptation and a trap and into many foolish and harmful desires that plunge people into ruin and destruction. For the love of money is a root of all kinds of evil. Some people, eager for money, have wandered from the faith and pierced themselves with many griefs. But you, man of God, flee from all this, and pursue righteousness, godliness, faith, love, endurance and gentleness.

I didn't see that Scripture as pertaining to me, only to others. I did not give Jesus time to convict me on a daily basis.

I allowed my business to draw me away from my husband. I paid more attention to those in my organization than I did my own children. As a result, I became vulnerable to emotional infidelity.

Our daughter, Roby, who is now twenty-five, told me recently how, as a sophomore, she ran for class officer at Bothell High School. As she was telling me about the incredible speech she had given at the opening assembly, I thought, *You missed it. Where were you when she was growing up?* I hadn't even known what was going on in her life.

I promised my kids that when I made enough money, I'd spend more time with them. Of course, that day never came. At least ten family vacations never happened or were cancelled at the last minute because of my work.

It grieves me to say that three of our four kids loved the world more than they loved the Lord.

Chasing the American Dream has taken an awful toll on families. Women who aren't getting their needs met at home, or who have experienced tremendous wounding in their lives, seem to be especially attracted to multilevel marketing type businesses. Many women subconsciously cope with latent pain by spending most of their time working. I was one of those wounded women. I was so engrossed with building a business, I never gave the Lord a chance to walk me through the healing I so desperately needed.

QUESTIONS FOR PERSONAL REFLECTION OR
Small Group Study

---

1. "I focused on the exciting venture I was part of." Have you ever been drawn away from serving God by the excitement of a situation or adventure? Describe how this affected you in your business.

2. "I never stopped to quiet my soul to listen to God's voice and receive His instruction for the day. Because of my lack of Christian disciplines, I became susceptible to ungodly suggestions." Does this resonate with you? Have you been drawn away from God's plan because of a lack of Christian disciplines? How can you make a daily habit of drawing near to God an integral part of your life?

3. First Corinthians 10:12 says, "Let him who thinks he stands take heed lest he fall." How would you describe this verse within a setting of your business? Do you consider yourself immune to this truth?

4. "Matthew 5:28 points out, if you've lusted in your mind, you're just as guilty." How does this happen in the business world? Have you seen this play out in your own life? Has the drive to satisfy your dream made you susceptible?

CHAPTER SEVEN

SELLING THE DREAM

Chuck and I used to hold weekly "opportunity meetings." In these high-powered gatherings, designated leaders presented business opportunities in a way that worked people into a selling frenzy. The idea was to get them signed up that night and motivated to really "do it!" Sometimes we'd have meetings two or three times a week to capitalize on the momentum.

There are many books on how to be successful in network marketing. Chuck and I even authored a few. The experts all teach the best way to get people excited about an opportunity is to show them graphically how bad their current situation is. Then you offer to rescue them from the terrible financial trap they are in with your product or business opportunity.

To raise dissatisfaction with the status quo, you must knock down the credibility of corporate America, traditional small business, and franchises. If you can make these look bad, your solution will look good in contrast.

When we believed in the free enterprise system, we were convinced that a regular job, where you have to punch a time clock and be submitted to a boss, was the worst kind of life. It had no freedom, no independence, no joy, no future. In our presentations we'd raise fear that with an ordinary job, a person would never have enough money to get ahead. We reminded them of the "important" things in life: a big house, a fancy car, private schools, and fun family vacations.

Chuck and I created a slide show for our opportunity meetings. It started out asking, "Whatever happened to the American Dream?" It then painted the following picture of discontent and frustration: "Back in the early 1900s only 10 percent of the population had to work for an employer. Since then, almost all of us have been sold on the idea that a steady job in a large company is the way to achieve our dreams. We call that the corporate dream, and it's a lie! It is a deception designed to benefit those organizations for which we work."

With rhythmic precision, the slide show progressed to talk about the corporate ladder and how few positions there are at the top. "If anyone is going to get those positions, it will be a relative of the owner. What about all the politics you have to play to move up? The big corporations make you promises and then never keep them. You can't put your trust in them."

When insecurity about the future had been raised, we'd let them know that they could trust network marketing. It wasn't just a way. It was held up as the only way.

We'd ask, "Who dictates the kind of car you drive? The kind of home you live in? The kind of education you give your children? The amount of money you're able to give to the ministries or charities of your choice? The kind of vacations you take? And how about retirement?"

The answer to those questions was designed to create discontent and insecurity in the audience. "Your boss determines those things by what he pays you!"

By this time, people felt dissatisfied and angry about their bosses, their jobs, and their lack of financial freedom. Then we would zero in by asking questions like "Are you keeping your head above debt level? Are you living from paycheck to paycheck? Is it ever going to get any better?" We'd raise the possibility of mergers, takeovers, cutbacks, layoffs, transfers, demotions, and unfair evaluations. "Would a cold, calculated decision to eliminate your job be devastating to you?"

We really rubbed it in by suggesting that most couples have handled these problems by sending Mom back to work. When she's away from the house eight to ten hours a day, the children no longer have the advantage of a full-time mother at home. She misses the experiences of helping the children develop, and by the time she does get home from work, she's tired and has to play catch-up.

"Once you calculate all the taxes, babysitters, second car payment and maintenance, lunches out, and additional wardrobe," we'd point out, "Mom is only making about one dollar an hour to help pay the bills."

Then, just before we made our case for network marketing, we would throw some salt in the wound. The next slide would read:

The majority of Americans:

- Never establish an emergency savings fund
- Never get out of debt
- Can't afford to buy a house
- Can't afford to start their own business
- Can't afford to send their children to private school or college
- Can't fund the ministries or charities of their choice
- End up in poverty in their old age
- Die never having enough money to make their dreams come true.

The next slide confirmed those statements with statistics. Out of every 100 people at age 65:

- 54 percent have to live off others
- 36 percent are dead
- 5 percent are still working
- 4 percent are well off
- 1 percent are wealthy

And then the kicker: "How are you doing so far?"

By this time, every person in the audience was dissatisfied and discontent.

Now, don't get me wrong. I'm not saying the statistics aren't true. Many people are unhappy with their current employment. But what if our job situation is just one of many ways the Lord purifies our motives and teaches us to be obedient and thankful in all circumstances? What if He is using our jobs to make us more like Him—meek and humble?

In *Hearing God*, Peter Lord says:

> God is more interested in the development of your character than he is in changing your circumstances. God's committal to us centers around conformity to Christ. God is not interested in helping us develop a philosophy of escape from problems by more dependence on Him. He wants us to have a philosophy of triumph in overcoming problems.
>
> Therefore, you can expect that God's wisdom to you will deal more with the development of your character than with circumstances. He knows that when Christ is in charge in you,

the circumstances will change you. He may or may not change the circumstance.

Are you asking God to give you a new job because of adverse conditions where you are at present? Often it is not his will to change your circumstances. He uses those circumstances to transform you![1]

I cannot deny that the presentations we led were calculated to make people covet what someone else has and become discontent with what they have. We were not living by Colossians 3:5, which says, "Put to death therefore what is earthly in you: sexual immorality, impurity, passion, evil desire, and covetousness, which is idolatry" (ESV).

Stacking the Odds in Our Favor

Our presentations didn't stop there. We would then present the options available to people in business today.

"How costly is it to start your own business? Buy a franchise? Become a doctor or lawyer?" We showed how the odds are stacked against an individual since 90 percent of all small businesses fail in the first five years.

Next we examined the option of living off investment income, showing the discouraging fact that in order to generate $3,000 a month in interest, half a million dollars would need to be invested early on.

"It's obvious," we'd say, "that there is only one way to make it, to survive, to be free, independent, and successful. That is to get involved with our network marketing program! The cost is minimal to get started. You could work part time and begin by sponsoring others and helping them learn to sponsor others. You develop a network that pays you residual income for life."

To really make it stick, we asked people how they would spend all the extra money they would be making with our company. Pictures of new houses, private schools, boats and other recreational vehicles, safaris and cruises, and savings accounts would further entice involvement. I've heard of some organizations where the men have their wives parade around in designer clothes and expensive jewelry to get the women excited.

The rest of the presentation was a smorgasbord of dreams and fantasies. "If you sponsor five people, and they each sponsor five, and they each do the same, pretty soon you have thousands upon thousands in your downline and you'll make really big bucks."

As I think back on how we motivated people toward greed, Proverbs 15:2 burns in my heart: "The tongue of the wise uses knowledge rightly, but the mouth of fools pours forth foolishness."

What impressive presentations do not say is that a very small percentage of people who get involved in MLM make any substantial money. Significantly fewer than 20 percent even make a profit. That means there are a lot of people losing money for everyone who makes some!

Pushing the Right Buttons

We built our empire in an opportunity meeting format. It was full of testimonials about how great the products were, how the products saved people's lives, and how easy it was to make thousands with hardly any work. Recently I received a letter in the mail with the same message as our slide show.

Dear Fellow Entrepreneur,

Do you know what "residual income" is? I didn't until two-and-a-half years ago. At that time we were broke! My husband hurt his back and with a ninth-grade education, it was hard for him to find a job. I was taught you had to go to school, get a job, slave for 30 years and hope for the best. In September of 1992, we began working a homebased business. I was extremely skeptical. Nonetheless, we worked hard, met a lot of people, had a lot of fun and made a lot of money.

Last Christmas, we went on a month-long vacation to the Caribbean. When we returned, there was a check in the mailbox for over $9000. That is residual income! Today, we live in a "street of dreams" home on 10 acres. We drive the cars of our choice. We have all the toys.

Two days before receiving that letter, I got this fax:

Dear Friend:

We have recently discovered (by complete accident) what is the most incredible opportunity we have ever seen. We have made a lot of money in two tremendous businesses, but never, not ever have we seen a more powerful and quicker way to make an incredible sum of money. If you would like to make in excess of $10,000 in the next 2-4 weeks, please call me immediately. P.S. My associate and good friend made $116,000 his very first month! We're going to take this to the top and a lot of very good people are going along with us! Call me A.S.A.P.

Notice the same buttons being pushed, making people think that being committed to an employer and being content with the income they have seems like a stupid, narrow, weak attitude?

In my early years of involvement in financial services, the coach told us that if we made $50-100,000 a year and produced a big organization with a lot of sales, we would be somebody. We'd be number one! If we weren't excited and motivated, making lots of contacts, sales, and money, we would be nobody—we'd be defeated!

It grieves my heart to see how these organizations and their inspirational leaders mold us into thinking that success in their program is the ultimate goal for which to live. Hebrews 13:5 says:

> Let your conduct be without covetousness; be content with such things as you have. For He Himself has said, "I will never leave you nor forsake you."

Fake It Till You Make It

In my first experience with multilevel marketing, everything was based on how much money we made. Chuck and I didn't have the cash to buy the trappings of success, but we believed we could do this business. So we leased what we felt we needed to look successful and to attract good people. The idea was that if they looked at us and wanted what we had, they'd likely join our team.

The coaches didn't exactly tell us that. But they did parade successful recruiters across the screen and on the stage who had all these things. So naturally, we assumed that in order to do what they were doing we needed to look like they did.

When Chuck and I moved to Seattle from the Los Angeles area, I opened a 3,500-square-foot office, then leased expensive office equipment, huge plants, paintings, and wall murals so we would look successful. I drove a red Merkur that went so fast I found it almost impossible to stay under the speed limit. Of course, I needed the toys: car phone, pager, cell phone. We lived in a 4,000-square-foot English Tudor dream house. Everything we had was obtained "zero down" with the smallest payments we could get. We financed what we wanted over four-, five-, or six-year leases.

Again, the coach never encouraged us to go into debt. In fact, he preached, "Make money and save money." But the pressure to create a successful image toned down his admonitions to keep expenses low. I had learned as a young girl the way to get attention and recognition was to compete and win, so my deep fear of being rejected fueled a lot of these unhealthy business practices.

We were encouraged to build relationships with our recruits by having them join us for a gourmet meal and spending time "selling them the dream." Almost every night of the week we had a different couple over for dinner. We would "wine them and dine them," asking thought-provoking questions like "What's your dream, Joe? What is it that you want this business to do for you?"

As I look back on those days, I am ashamed to admit that I cannot remember one time that I employed the gift of hospitality to love on friends, relatives, or acquaintances for any other reason. All our activities were designed to build our business. We would treat them like royalty while the notice from the gas company threatening disconnection lay on my desk in the other room!

One evening we went out to a fancy meal and a stage play with our newest recruit and his fiancé. They had been given free tickets to the play and we were "going Dutch" for the dinner. Chuck and I were so broke we couldn't afford a meal. We had seven dollars to our name. We each ordered a salad, saying, "Oh, we're not really hungry."

I wonder now if they saw the yearning in our eyes as we watched them eat their New York steaks. I was making over $100,000 a year, but I was spending $150,000 just to keep the thing going!

I had a good friend who was consumed by looking successful and creating the image of prosperity. She opened a swank office in a suburb of Seattle with designer colors, high-end furnishings, and the hottest office equipment available. Since Laurie was married to a doctor with a thriving practice, she was able to create a smoke screen of affluence by using his money and credit. For the entire time I knew her in business, she gave the appearance of being successful. In reality, she was spending far more than she made just to keep up the front.

Mark was so intent on making it in the business that he spent all his money advertising, taking people out to expensive restaurants, and acting like a "high roller." All the while Mark's wife, Marva, and their three children under the age of five were constantly stranded at home with no car, no money, no diapers, and no food. All the family's income was being squandered on the business and on looking successful.

In pretending to be something we are not and striving to get rich quick, we build our lives on shaky ground.

Deceptive Practices

I learned from my coach that a great way to find prospects for the business was to attend events and gatherings in the community, such as my children's Little League games. We were taught to start a conversation with someone who looked like a good potential recruit. The more questions we asked about them, the more they would enjoy talking about themselves, their jobs, their families, etc. Sooner or later they would ask us, "What do you do for a living?" That was what we were waiting for—the opening to recruit them into our business!

Let's face it. No one wants to be sold anything. If you appeal to folks with "I'd like to show you a way to make some extra money," you'll probably scare them off. A better method is to ask a question. I'd say something like this: "I know you're a busy person and probably wouldn't need anything like this, but do you know anyone who might want to make an extra five hundred to a thousand dollars a month, working part time?"

At least half of the time, the person is going to say, "I wouldn't mind earning that much extra money myself!"

The Dangling Carrot

A friend of mine recently shared how his daughter and her husband had been recruited into a high-powered business after graduating from a Christian college. The parents, wanting them to be successful, loaned the young couple thousands of dollars to help "build their business." They later learned the money was spent on an expensive car, $300 shoes, and the like.

The daughter convinced her parents that she was building on a firm foundation. But the company she was part of was dangling an irresistible carrot. The top twenty-four people in the company would receive lifetime income. If they worked hard for the next two or three years, they would be set for life! Before long the young couple had racked up over $100,000 in bills flying all over the country "building their business." Today they are divorced and have filed for bankruptcy.

Part of "selling the dream" would be convincing people to make emotional decisions to get involved.

"If you don't start now, think of all the people you know that someone else might recruit! Why, last week a guy in the meeting brought someone he had recently met at church. He was so excited about this opportunity he signed up on the spot! His sister had been at a meeting the week before and was still trying to decide whether to do the business or not. Boy, did she regret not signing up and getting to him first!"

We never suggested that anyone ask the Lord if this was something he or she was supposed to be involved with. Our vocabulary never included the admission that, while the program might be OK for one person, it may not be right for another. The frenzy to build, build, build, and block out all negatives kept us channeling our energies into signing up everyone we came in contact with.

In all sales programs you're taught to "get 'em while they're hot!" God's will never seems to come up as a consideration. I can't remember one instance when anyone took the time to find out if it was God's will for his or her life.

I now regret every time someone joined the business because I talked them into it.

> Proverbs 19:1–2 says:
>
> Better is a poor person who walks in his integrity than a person who is perverse in speech and is a fool. Also it is not good for a person to be without knowledge, and one who hurries his footsteps errs. (NASB)
>
> The Living Bible translates that verse this way:
>
> Better be poor and honest than rich and dishonest. It is dangerous and sinful to rush into the unknown. (TLB)

Today I get at least five phone calls a week from fellow believers trying to recruit my husband and me into a new program. My response is always "Friend, I know what you're doing. And I am not a prospect for your new business. I do not endorse the business model of recruiting a downline to generate your financial future, so nothing you say will change my mind. I have been down that road and been convicted that it does not honor God."

Proverbs 28:19–20 says:

He who tills his land will have plenty of bread, but he who follows frivolity will have poverty enough! A faithful man will abound with blessings, but he who hastens to be rich will not go unpunished.

I am convicted by the words of Jesus in Luke 16:13–15:

"No servant can serve two masters; for either he will hate the one and love the other, or else he will be loyal to the one and despise the other. You cannot serve God and mammon."

Now the Pharisees, who were lovers of money, also heard all these things, and they derided Him. And He said to them, "You are those who justify yourselves before men, but God knows your hearts. For what is highly esteemed among men is an abomination in the sight of God."

Making big money and becoming financially independent may be highly esteemed by men, but letting our hearts be consumed by that pursuit is an abomination in God's sight.

QUESTIONS FOR PERSONAL REFLECTION OR
Small Group Study

1. "God is more interested in the development of your character than he is in changing your circumstances." How have you seen God use your circumstances to mold your character? Does it create a sense of security in you?

2. "Fake It Till You Make It." This can be applied to many areas of life. Have you been tempted to do this? What was it you had to fake? How did it work out for you?

3. "I had learned as a child that the way to get attention and recognition was to compete and win." Did you strive for attention and recognition as a child? How does this play into what you strive for in your business? Do you see this as one of Satan's methods of distraction? Explain how this makes you feel.

4. Proverbs 19:1–2 says: "Better be poor and honest than rich and dishonest. It is dangerous and sinful to rush into the unknown." How does this proverb speak into your business practices? Have you experienced this truth in the way you move forward in your decisions? What was the result?

5. Jesus in Luke 16:13–15: "No servant can serve two masters; for either he will hate the one and love the other, or else he will be loyal to the one and despise the other. You cannot serve God and mammon." Who are you serving? What happens when you try to divide your loyalties? Describe the tension it creates in your business.

CHAPTER EIGHT

MIRACLE WORKERS AND FALSE PROFITS

Salespeople are an interesting bunch. When we buy into a product or company, we go all out to get everyone we know excited about it.

One company I represented had an herbal product that garnered amazing testimonials, everything from deliverance from cigarettes, arthritis healed, blood pressure down to normal, and asthma gone. When a friend of mine told her pastor husband about the meeting, he responded, "Hey, if you've got that product, who needs Jesus?"

That is a really good question! With products that seemingly create life-changing results, we begin worshipping the product and its creator. Our zeal is directed toward getting people healed by the product we sell. The salesperson considers himself a miracle worker.

Our focus is misdirected. Consider James 5:13–15:

> Is anyone among you suffering? Let him pray. Is anyone cheerful? Let him sing psalms. Is anyone among you sick? Let

him call for the elders of the church, and let them pray over him, anointing him with oil in the name of the Lord. And the prayer of faith will save the sick, and the Lord will raise him up. And if he has committed sins, he will be forgiven.

Why are we always rushing to find a "miracle cure" instead of rushing to the Master Physician?

Gimmicks in Disguise

In sales, you have to believe in what you're selling. Once you do, you learn all the right buttons to push to convince someone to purchase your product. Since the product fills a need, it's OK to manipulate people to get them to buy it!

Many of the best sales training seminars are based on the following techniques:

1. Build rapport with the customer.

The unsuspecting customers are warmed by your friendly manner of complimenting them on their house, their pets, whatever you can find to identify with. Mirror their body language. If they cross their legs, cross your legs; if they fold their arms and sit back, do the same. Spend a lot of time chitchatting, becoming "friends" to make them comfortable with you. Show them you "care" about them. (If we really cared about them, we would be sharing the Lord with them.)

2. Find out what your customer's hot buttons are.

Learn what is important to your customers, what their fears are, what makes them happy, what frustrates them, and what their goals and dreams are. Then you have the ammunition you need to take the sales process in the direction you want.

3. Gear your presentation to make your product or opportunity push your customer's hot buttons.

Control the conversation. At the appropriate time, throw into the sales presentation an explanation of how your product will give your customers what they want, relieve them of frustration, help them achieve their goal, whatever. "Go for the close" when you push the hot button, and use the assumptive close: why they'd be crazy not to want to do this!

The Personality Test Gimmick

Years before I became a Christian, I was involved in Scientology. I worked in the department that recruited new people into the organization and got them signed up for their first course.

One gimmick the Church of Scientology used was a personality test. After a prospective client took this test, it was graded and all the areas where he scored low were highlighted. These areas, we were trained to tell him, were ruining his life. Then the close. No matter what the perceived problem area was, we told him that Scientology would help him handle it. There were always deep emotions attached to the area of the person's life that was in shambles. The hope that Scientology could fix that problem would suck him into spending hundreds and sometimes thousands of dollars to "get better."

This technique is one of the most successful forms of sales. Without being a high-pressure, arm-twisting kind of salesperson, you can subtly get your customer doing what you want him to do.

These gimmicks are nothing less than manipulation.

A sales trainer once told me numerous stories of how he went through this three-step process and closed the sale, recruiting "big fish." One time he was selling a limited partnership opportunity to a very wealthy businessman on the East Coast. As he wined and dined this man in a dark corner of a prestigious hotel lounge, he learn about his weaknesses, frustrations, hopes, and dreams. He then used his ammunition to turn the meeting into a $100,000 commission for himself by painting a picture of stress-free living through income from the limited partnership. He pushed all his buttons and got what he wanted—his commission!

This type of manipulation devalues people made in God's image. In fact, they become merely a prize for the one who can successfully master the circumstances to his or her advantage.

My father told me he had a line that always got him in the door when he was selling encyclopedias. He pushed all the buttons he was trained to, subtly insinuating that if the parents really loved their children, they would give them the gift of knowledge. He recounted stories of single mothers on welfare to whom he sold a $500 set of encyclopedias, all because he was such an incredible closer.

New Age Success Techniques

Many Christians are opening the door to the enemy by using new age techniques to ensure success in multilevel marketing organizations. Almost all consumer direct-sales companies suggest their representatives read *Think and Grow Rich* by Napoleon Hill. Most use it for its helpful goal-setting techniques, but buried away in the last part of the book are rituals of calling up the wisdom of great dead men like George Washington. This sounds to me like some kind of seance.

Or how about visualizing yourself driving the car of your dreams into the circular driveway in front of your 6,000-square-foot mansion? Many leaders suggest that their people go to a Lexus or Mercedes car lot and test drive their favorite new model. As they drive around, they are to drink in the feel and sensation of driving this luxury vehicle. Afterward, they are encouraged to recreate in their minds the positive image of them driving that car. In this way, they are told, their visualization will eventually become a reality. "If you can believe it, you can achieve it" is a favorite slogan in MLM.

One Christian MLM leader I know used to suggest that everyone close their eyes and see themselves standing in front of a room full of people, with the idea that those people were all in their organization.

I've recently read the literature for a Christian MLM where people supposedly earn money by sponsoring a needy child. Only 25 percent of the revenue actually goes to the agency providing support to these children. What disturbed me the most about this program was reading about their "Wealth Builders Series" available in their lending library. Through this program you can buy or borrow the "best books on success in the country." When I saw they included books like *Think and Grow Rich* by Napoleon Hill, I was really concerned.

This company is using the strategy to link a worthwhile project, like helping children, with getting rich quick. They make it seem godly because the money being spent is going to a worthy cause. Many Christians are being caught unaware in their drive to succeed.

There are even books that insinuate that Jesus was in favor of multilevel marketing. One is titled *Jesus Was a Double-Diamond*. Yes, Jesus was a great example of networking. He told twelve people, who told others, who told more, and today we have millions of Christians. The glaring difference is that in all the "telling," there was no financial reward involved. It comes down to heart motives. The motives of the people who first shared the gospel were pure, even if man's pride and basic sin nature sometimes got in the way. When the bottom-line is making money, you'd better watch out.

When salespeople consider themselves miracle workers, they take the glory away from God. Those who exploit others for their own selfish gain are not following the Lord. Where are the prophets in our day who will stand up for truth and righteousness?

QUESTIONS FOR PERSONAL REFLECTION OR *Small Group Study*

1. "Hey, if you've got that product, who needs Jesus?" Most of us have fallen for the lie that something material can ultimately satisfy us. Think about ways you have fallen for this lie. Describe how you overcame it or found yourself trapped.

2. Manipulation is one of Satan's tactics. In truth, manipulation devalues people made in God's image. Describe a time when you've been manipulated. Did this experience cause you to feel devalued? How did you rise above a time when you have been a victim to this behavior?

3. "'If you can believe it, you can achieve it' is a favorite slogan in MLM." Have you heard this within your business model? Have you ever said it? Describe the danger found within the use of this phrase.

4. "Jesus was a great example of networking. He told twelve people, who told others, who told more, and today we have millions of Christians. The glaring difference is that in all the 'telling,' there was no financial reward involved. It comes down to heart motives." Can you articulate the motives that dictate your life? How is that seen in your business? What would those who work with you say about the motives of your heart?

CHAPTER NINE

IT ALL CAME CRASHING DOWN

In June of 1994, I saw Chuck off at the airport for his flight to Virginia Beach, where he was going to attend the Christian Broadcasting Network's annual Victory Over Vietnam Conference. I was glad he was getting away, as I thought for sure God had something to say to my husband about the restoration of his vision for his ministry to Vietnam veterans.

But God had a different agenda. His plan in sending Chuck to CBN was to get me alone for a whole weekend so He could put His finger on some areas of sin in my life. He needed my full attention so He could convict me on my heart motives.

An overwhelming urge to pray pushed me to my knees—someplace I hadn't been in a very long time. As I spent an extended period in quiet prayer, the Lord took my thoughts back to July of 1991. Flipping through my journal from that time period took my breath away. As I reread the marching orders the Lord had given me, a wave of conviction washed over me. I had been in complete disobedience by getting back into MLM. God had told me what He wanted me to do and I had gone off in another direction just because it sounded good. I had assumed that because I saw an open door, I should go through it. The Lord made it undeniably clear that just because that door was open did not mean He wanted me to walk through it!

God's Convicting Power

The new high-tech communication business we had jumped into seemed to have all the ingredients the other company lacked. But the Lord showed me that motives, not good management or great products, were the issue.

Stress and anxiety overtook me as I thought of the struggle Chuck and I were having to rebuild our organizations with the new company. Business was not growing as fast as it needed to in order to cover all the overhead.

When I stopped and listened to God, He immediately directed me to a book in our bookcase titled *Men's Manual: Financial Freedom* by Bill Gothard. Thinking I'd find some suggestions for the problem of insufficient finances, I turned to the section on financial freedom principles. The words I read pierced my heart.

Gothard lists God's four purposes for money:

1. To provide basic needs
2. To confirm direction
3. To give to Christians
4. To illustrate God's power[2]

Purpose number 2 jumped off the page at me. "Money, or lack thereof, is God's way of confirming His direction for our lives."[3]

If people used credit to get involved in our new business, they were bypassing God's caution sign. If the money wasn't available, that was His way of saying no. We were suggesting and even encouraging Christians to "make it happen" on their own without God's blessing or confirmation.

My heart was heavy with conviction as I continued to look through the large leatherbound book. In the section on "Developing Sales Resistance," I found a definition that brought me godly sorrow.

> SALES RESISTANCE: Being content with food and clothing, using and caring for the possessions that we have, and keeping our focus on the purpose for which God made us.[4]

Gothard defined alluring advertising as "carefully planned appeals to our human weaknesses designed to make us discontent with what we have so that we can rationalize buying things that we know we do not need and should not have."[5]

At that moment a powerful conviction swept over me. The previous three years were like a weight on my back. I recognized I had been full of rebellion, disobedience, and sin.

As I read on, the Lord showed me all the ways I was promoting sinful behavior in the manner I did business. The list of subtle advertising tactics jumped off the page:

- Creating discontentment
- Promoting an independent spirit
- Depending on human reasoning
- Appealing to the lust of the eyes
- Offering fulfillment apart from God
- Denying the product's weakest points.[6]

That is exactly what we were doing in our business and in every sales organization I'd ever been involved with!

As the weight of what I had done pressed down on me, I felt ashamed. The Lord did an instant replay of every advertisement I'd ever written for the radio ad campaigns. He reminded me of every script I'd ever crafted for the voice-mail message people heard when they called in for information. He took me back to the way I'd developed the slide-show presentation and every other sales tool I had created. I saw those tactics in every promotional campaign I had ever done, even after I became a Christian.

My conscience had been activated, and I could no longer compromise or straddle the fence by being deceitful or dishonest.

But the Lord wasn't done with me yet. He showed me how I had been exploiting my God-given ability to motivate believers for the wrong ends—encouraging them to make money and build a successful business rather than influencing them to a closer walk with Jesus.

Facing the Obvious

The next Monday morning I was sitting in my office feeling emotionally wrung out when Jo walked in. She looked at me with concern and said, "Can we go to lunch? I know you have lots on your mind. Maybe it'll help to talk."

I knew God had sent her and I was going to have to spill out all that He had revealed to me. I was so used to being the strong one, the leader for everyone, I was taking a risk in revealing my heart. But I knew Jo's sensitivity to the things of God and believed she would not condemn me.

As we were going through the buffet line at the pizza place, confusion brought me to a place of being nervous about sharing what

I'd been coming to grips with. But I couldn't turn back now. I blurted it all out. Tears ran down my cheeks and I mopped them up with the napkins at the table. Seeing my sin the way God did overwhelmed me with godly sorrow.

The conviction of God collided with a sense of responsibility. I became terribly conflicted. "I can't let the shareholders down. I have to keep it together so people won't lose their investments. I need to continue being the leader and motivating the troops." Even as I said those words, they sounded foolish in my ears. How could I control everything when God wanted to be in control?

Jo made me face the obvious. "Give it up, Athena. You can't try to save the corporation or keep the organization going if God is shutting that door. Why don't you just let Him do whatever He wants to do?"

Beginning to loosen my grip on the situation, I knew she was right.

"Get rid of the office," she suggested. "Scale back, then let it grow slowly and see what God does."

Her idea seemed impossible. My palms became sweaty and a knot formed in my stomach. Releasing the control I had was frightening, yet as I entertained the thought, a burden rolled off my shoulders.

When I picked Chuck up from the airport, I told him what had been happening to me and what the Lord was showing me, then asked him what he thought.

"Shut it down!" he wholeheartedly agreed.

I had to tell my associates I was going to quit being their leader and let God direct the course of the business and its outcome. But what then? They wouldn't all be as understanding as Jo was.

Would they feel like they were being abandoned? The idea of letting them down punched me in the gut.

The Lord kept reassuring me, *You have to unchain yourself.* With conviction, I decided to be obedient.

At that moment I remembered the vow I made when I was nineteen years old.

After falling in love at that young age, I felt taken advantage of when the relationship ended. I promised myself I would never let anyone use me again. I hardened my heart and subconsciously set out to live life on my own terms.

The pendulum swung and I became the user. My MO was to control every situation and not let myself be vulnerable. After all, people couldn't be trusted, and I had to make sure I never got hurt again.

Now I was about to tell people who trusted me I was not going to be their leader anymore. No doubt there would be hard feelings. But I had to follow God's direction, no matter the personal cost.

The first step was to tell the board I was finished and let them know what I thought we should do with the center.

"I'm sorry, you guys. But I just can't do this anymore. I don't want to disappoint you, but I believe the Lord is asking me to step away. I think we should close this place and see what happens. You'll have to care for your people and run your own meetings."

Their faces registered dismay, worry, and shock.

Because I had peace that I was doing the right thing, I didn't give in to guilt and try to make everyone feel better by saying I'd take care of the details.

Still, I knew this was going to be a difficult transition for me. My future was uncertain. I wasn't even sure who I was anymore, for my identity had been so wrapped up in my leadership position.

The World's Redemption

I was scheduled to attend a leadership training session in Palm Springs for the high-tech business I was working with. I couldn't get out of the commitment because the company had paid my way.

During the final phase of the training, each leader was asked to stand up in front of the rest of the attendees and practice his or her inspirational speech. Then we were to go back to our teams and motivate them to greater achievements. Which, of course, would result in more income for everyone.

Now that I clearly understood the abomination of the business methods I had involved myself with, I felt sick to my stomach.

It was Sunday morning, and instead of being in church worshipping, these people, many of them Christians, were worshipping the almighty dollar.

Feeling disconnected, I watched a former pastor stand and "share his heart." He preached that redemption could come through fame, fortune, and success. Shrinking down in my chair I prayed, *Oh, God, forgive us for being so deceived!*

There was no going back now. No matter what my family's financial condition was, I never again wanted anything that was not God's perfect will for me. I had lived for years following one good idea after another, and many of them paid off. But just because they made money, didn't mean they were God's best for my life. Proverbs 14:12 flashed through my mind: "There is a way that seems right to a man, but its end is the way of death."

Because I hadn't committed myself to prayer and waiting for confirmation and peace, seeking godly counsel from those to whom I was accountable, I left myself open to deception. Those three years of disobedience almost cost me my marriage, my children, my spiritual life, and my integrity. But praise God, His mercies are new every morning (Lamentations 3:22–33).

> If we say that we have fellowship with Him, and walk in darkness, we lie and do not practice the truth. But if we walk in the light as He is in the light, we have fellowship with one another, and the blood of Jesus Christ His Son cleanses us from all sin. If we say that we have no sin, we deceive ourselves, and the truth is not in us. If we confess our sins, He is faithful and just to forgive us our sins and to cleanse us from all unrighteousness. (1 John 1:6–9)

My Deliverance

After returning home from Palm Springs, I went through three months of depression and confusion. I felt useless. I had no mission in life. I felt like a loser. Many days I wore my blue bathrobe until late afternoon, my hair a mess, my heart feeling void.

Several people called, asking me what was wrong. I couldn't explain what I still didn't really have a grasp of myself, so I just told them I was taking a leave of absence to deal with some family problems.

I tried to gracefully and gradually back out of the horrible situation I was stuck in. I served on the advisory council for the communications company. Every other week we had nationwide conference calls that lasted two to three hours. I was so physically drained and emotionally decimated, I had to drag myself out of bed for those calls. I had no interest in the business, no desire to compete or achieve or impress anyone. I felt hollow and phony and like I had nothing to offer.

I stopped answering phone calls and refused to see anyone. Chuck had to take care of all the household chores.

Jo came by in the middle of the day and found me lying on the couch in my bathrobe, immobilized. She talked with me and prayed for me even though I was too depressed to pray for myself. Sensing the dark night of the soul I was in, she stood in the gap on my behalf.

Eventually, I felt strong enough to give voice to my pleas.

"Oh, Lord, create in me a heart that hates the things You hate and loves the things You love. Help me to be excited about Your kingdom, not worldly projects and ventures. Let me value people for who they are, not what I can get out of them. Remove the stronghold in my life that has caused me to love the things of this world more than I love You."

God answered those prayers.

One sunny day in late August, I lay on my bed and sobbed uncontrollably for hours. The pain was so intense I could hardly stand it. But when my wailing ended, I felt cleansed. As if something that was lodged inside my being had been stripped out. In its place was a peace, a fulfillment, a true longing for the things of God. I had been transformed by the power of the Holy Spirit. My urge to be important disappeared. I actually wanted to listen for God's will and be obedient to it without compulsive dysfunctional behavior getting in the way.

God had done a new work in me, and I was amazed.

During my three months of darkness, as my income dwindled away to nothing, Chuck picked up the slack by rustling up photography and book publishing jobs. I tried to help him, but I wasn't worth much. By some miracle, we managed to make our house payments each month.

Tentmaking Together

When I felt ready to work again, Chuck and I spent a season praying and fasting, asking God to show us what we should do to make ends meet. Kneeling together at the edge of our bed, we pleaded, "Oh, Lord, show us Your will for our lives!"

He made it very clear that He wanted us to work together as a couple. He brought the thought to my mind that if I helped Chuck with the publishing venture, we could make ends meet.

Instead of blurting it out immediately, I waited to see if the Lord would speak the same thing to my husband's heart. A day or two later, Chuck told me, "I feel like the Lord wants us to focus on the publishing business. And we need to work together. No more 'lone ranger' stuff." Confirmation received!

The Lord put a deep desire in our hearts to see the Word of God pour into people's lives through the printed page. We narrowed our focus to working with Christian writers. Helping them publish their testimonies, teachings, or personal experiences in book form would be our ministry, and we trusted this would generate enough income to provide for our family.

We had published a dozen books over the previous seven years. By doing this full time, we could be available for the children and serve the body of Christ. We established rates that were significantly less than the competition but enough that we could still make a living at this.

Roby Hears the Still, Small Voice

Our eldest daughter got saved shortly after Christmas in 1986. But while Chuck and I were separately doing our things, we were too busy to nurture Roby and disciple her in the ways of the Lord. Because she never learned how to hear God's voice, the enemy deceived her and she started backsliding.

When Chuck and I walked away from the world and got sold out for Jesus, this created a huge wedge between us and Roby.

As the Lord turned my heart toward my children, I daily begged God to draw our children back to Himself, asking Jesus to make Himself real to them in such a way that they could no longer deny Him.

Roby spent a year in the Caribbean running from God and trying to find happiness in the world. Just before Christmas of 1995, she hit the skids. She called Chuck and tearfully told him she had no job, no car, no future. Everything in her life was falling apart.

"Come on home, honey," he suggested. "You can stay here as long as you need to."

We had just finished publishing Robert Andrew's excellent book titled *The Family, God's Weapon for Victory*. While reading it, we were convicted that we had not protected our daughter from the enemy's ploy to pull her away from the Lord. Now we wanted to do what we could to create an environment of restoration.

When Roby first came home, she was distant and hesitant around us. She didn't want to be preached to. She just wanted to get back on her feet. Through a series of circumstances, the Lord spoke to her in ways no man could orchestrate. She knew God was calling her. He made Himself real to her. She could no longer run. Her heart softened, and shortly after Christmas she recommitted her life to the Lord.

Yet she continued to struggle. The enemy fought hard to gain back the ground he had lost.

One night, as we were sitting in the living room talking about the things of the Lord, Chuck and I shared with Roby how important it is to listen for God's voice. She asked how we knew when we were hearing it.

"Roby," Chuck explained, "it's not some audible voice that booms down from the clouds. It's a still, small voice inside your heart. Sometimes it seems like your own voice, but you can feel in your heart that He is speaking to you."

Her eyes lit up. "That's God's voice? I never realized that!" She couldn't wait to get to her room so she could have a conversation with the Lord.

What we saw over the next few days was nothing short of miraculous. Roby's countenance was completely transformed. She became a new person. The nervous anxiety was gone. She was filled with that peace that passes all understanding (Philippians 4:6–7). She basked in the love that Jesus poured into her as He told her how much He loved her and that He had a plan for her life.

Oh, what a joy to see our prayers answered!

Roby is still growing by leaps and bounds, and her spiritual walk is deepening every day. The Lord is using her to minister to our other children, and I have hope that He will do the same for them. Our God is able!

Every month God brought in enough publishing jobs to pay our bills. We didn't do extravagant promotional campaigns to get business. We just put the word out in various areas and let the Lord direct people to us. We turned away manuscripts that could bring dishonor to the Lord, even if we needed the money. God always honored our integrity and sent us other jobs. With our new working situation, we were even able to volunteer in various ministry projects at our church.

God is faithful to provide for us when we trust and obey. He moves mountains when we depend on Him instead of our own ideas.

"For my thoughts are not your thoughts, nor are your ways My ways," says the Lord. "For as the heavens are higher than the earth, so are My ways higher than your ways, and My thoughts than your thoughts." (Isaiah 55:8–9)

The Lord taught us that in everything we do we must check our heart motives. We cannot operate in gray areas. Everything we do should be able to stand up to His holiness. We need to walk in the light as He is in the light (1 John 1:7). If we wait for Him to provide at all times and are faithful in the small things and wait for Him, He will prove Himself strong.

Every once in a while, we experience a season when there's no business coming in. That usually means God is trying to get my attention and reveal something I need to repent of or some area He wants to purify. I've learned to ask, "Lord, what are You trying to tell us?" Somehow, the lack of money always brings me to my knees. And my heavenly Father knows it.

QUESTIONS FOR PERSONAL REFLECTION OR
Small Group Study

1. "God needed my full attention so He could convict me on my heart motives." Does God have your full attention? If not, what do you think it would take for Him to get your full attention?

2. "I had been in complete disobedience by getting back into MLM." One doesn't have to be in complete disobedience to miss His instructions, disobeying "just a little" will do it. Are there areas in your business where you are not in complete obedience? What are those places that need to be surrendered to God?

3. "My conscience had been activated, and I could no longer compromise or straddle the fence by being deceitful or dishonest." Are you completely honest in your dealings? Are there areas where you know you are not being honest? What are you willing to do about it?

4. "Because I hadn't committed myself to prayer and waiting for confirmation and peace, seeking godly counsel from those to whom I was accountable, I left myself open to deception." How is your prayer life? Do you take time to intentionally listen to God? Do you have someone who is holding you accountable? What do you need to put in place so that you are not open to deception?

5. "That's God's voice? I never realized that!" Do you recognize God's voice? Are you in a position to hear Him?

CHAPTER TEN

THE BLINDING LIGHTS OF SUCCESS

When the Lord changed my heart, He also changed my definition of success. According to the *Concise Oxford Dictionary*, there are three definitions for success:

1. the achievement of an aim or purpose
2. the gaining of wealth or status
3. a person or thing that achieves success.[7]

Synonyms are victory, triumphs, prosperity, wealth, riches, opulence, affluence, best seller, sell out, winner, triumph, hit, smash, sensation.

The last two definitions represent the world's point of view. The first is most appropriate for Christians.

What is the meaning of *purpose*? Dictionary.com defines it as "the reason for which something exists or is done, made, used."[8]

For what were you made? Was it to get married, have a family, work at a job, build a business, earn a lot of money, own expensive possessions, take exotic vacations, and be financially independent?

Think about it. If that was our purpose in life, who would ever want to leave this earth?

When I was deeply entrenched in my climb to the top, the last thing I wanted was to die and go to heaven. Sitting around the throne and worshipping the Lord sounded boring when my eyes were on money and success.

Our main purpose in life is to do the will of the Father. When Christ ascended into heaven, He sent His Holy Spirit to live in us. We are the physical body of Christ on earth.

Our other purpose is to destroy the works of the enemy. 1 John 3:8 says, "The Son of God appeared for this purpose, to destroy the works of the devil" (NASB). If every day of our lives we make the choice to do the will of the Father and obey His Word, we will surely destroy the works of the enemy.

But it's hard to yield to what the Lord is asking of us if we surround ourselves with people who are consumed with the pursuit of worldly achievement.

After spending two years striving for fame in network marketing, Sandra and Jim realized that God was not calling them to that. They saw how easily they had been sucked in by listening to motivational recordings, reading books about financial success, and going to meetings meant to motivate them to make a lot of money.

Jim and Sandra decided they'd rather be broke and in God's will than do their own thing and be rolling in dough. They found purpose in where God planted them for work and even tried to reason with those they met who were consumed with the pursuit of worldly success. God provided for them and never let them down when they needed something.

"Life is short," Sandra says. "So we need to pray hard."

God created each of us to be unique individuals, and He has a plan for every life. If His plan for you is to be "salt and light" to other employees at a large corporation, doing anything else is disobedience.

The only way for a Christian to experience true success is to have a deep, personal relationship with the living God—to hear His voice and obey it. If we are focused on succeeding in business, we will find it very difficult to experience the deep walk with Jesus that we are called to have.

Whatever consumes our thoughts will grow strong in our lives. In Matthew 6:19–21, Jesus said:

> Do not lay up for yourselves treasures upon earth, where moth and rust destroy and where thieves break in and steal; but lay up for yourselves treasures in heaven, where neither moth nor rust destroys and where thieves do not break in or steal. For where your treasure is, there will your heart be also.

I have a friend who came to know the Lord through the business she was involved in. After hearing people testify how Jesus helped them make thousands of dollars a month, Maren thought, *Maybe I should give this Jesus a try.* At a weekend rally, she attended the Sunday service, where many of the top leaders in the organization shared their testimonies. An altar call closed the service, and she went forward to accept Christ.

After her decision, she felt like she could really go full bore in her pursuit because God was now on her side. Whenever she listened to a sermon or read the Word, she perked up over anything that seemed to encourage her in her business. She turned a deaf ear to any Scripture that seemed to correct or convict her. Following what she thought was God's call on her life, she neglected her family, and her marriage hit the rocks.

After years of being consumed with the pursuit of financial success, a near disaster brought Maren to her knees. She finally asked the Lord what He wanted her to do. And it wasn't what she'd been doing. She made the choice to walk away from the business and seek His will for her employment options.

Listen to the words of Job:

> If I have put my confidence in gold, and called fine gold my trust, if I have gloated because my wealth was great, and because my hand had obtained so much; if I have looked at the sun when it shone, or the moon going in splendor, and my heart was secretly enticed, and my hand threw a kiss from my mouth, that too would have been a guilty deed calling for judgment, for I would have denied God above. (Job 31:24–28 NASB)

Jeffrey was an on-fire Christian who achieved tremendous financial prosperity at a young age, quickly rising to the top of his company. He and his wife, Jennifer, live in a mansion complete with tennis and basketball courts, swimming pools, and maids' quarters. They own a Mercedes, a Bentley, a yacht, and a high-end RV. They also have a condo in the south of France, other properties in prime locations, a plush office, a personal library of antique books, and artwork worth hundreds of thousands of dollars.

Their children have everything they could ever want and are educated at the best schools. The family travels the world and stays in five-star hotels. Jeffrey and Jennifer give huge amounts of money to missions and their local church. They seem to live a fairy-tale life.

But what has this incredible financial success done to Jeffrey's spiritual life? The last time I saw him, he was seeing a psychologist twice a week, taking medication for depression, and drinking an entire bottle of expensive wine with dinner every evening. He has everything he could ever want—yet true fulfillment eludes him. He can't seem to find happiness or peace.

I often wonder what Jeffrey would hear if he asked the Lord what He wanted him to do with his life.

Do the blinding lights of financial abundance move you to close your eyes to the Word of God? Are you looking the other way as you chase after a worldly definition of success? When God convicts us of our sin, it can be oh so painful. But when we repent before Him, He washes that sin away. And He leads us from pain to joy.

It may be hard for you to imagine even wanting God to rule your life, letting go of the reins and letting Him have His way. I was always afraid that if I prayed, "Lord, Your will, not mine," He would make me give up all the things I loved. And sometimes He does! But when you surrender to Him and obey, the freedom you experience will be infinitely better than the adrenaline rush of anything the glamor and glitz of this world has to offer.

QUESTIONS FOR PERSONAL REFLECTION OR
Small Group Study

1. "When the Lord changed my heart, He also changed my definition of success." What is your definition of success? Discuss the changes you've experienced by following Jesus.

2. "Purpose: Dictionary.com defines it as "the reason for which something exists or is done, made, used." What do you think when you contemplate "purpose?" Can you define the specific purpose of your life?

3. "Our main purpose in life is to do the will of the Father." Do you agree? Does the path of your life demonstrate this? Why or why not?

4. "But it's hard to yield to what the Lord is asking of us if we surround ourselves with people who are consumed with the pursuit of worldly achievement." Is this true to your experience in business? Describe your experience with people who are consumed by worldly achievement.

5. "God created each of us to be unique individuals, and He has a plan for every life. If His plan for you is to be 'salt and light' to other employees at a large corporation, doing anything else is disobedience." How are you salt and light in your business? What is the response to the people you demonstrate these actions toward? Do the people you work with see this emulated within you? Explain.

6. "When God convicts us of our sin, it can be oh so painful. But when we repent before Him, He washes that sin away. And He leads us from pain to joy." Tell of a time when you were convicted yet experienced the joy of repentance.

CHAPTER ELEVEN

BODY COUNT IN THE CHURCH

It is time for the church to wake up. The number of lifeless, unproductive, lukewarm Christians is rising at an alarming rate. I believe much of this crisis is due to scores of Christians striving for money and worldly success.

As Christians, we are in a war. The enemy does not come at us dressed in a red suit and carrying a pitchfork. He conceals his position and attacks us in subtle ways. Over time, if we're not watchful for his deceptive suggestions, we will become lovers of the world instead of the sanctified, set-apart people we are chosen to be.

When the Lord first impressed upon me the need for this book, He showed me how rotten the elements at the core of the network marketing schemes are. Christians should not entangle themselves with something that is so opposed to the principles of God's Word.

I am often asked, "But can't a Christian ever be in MLM?" Many Christians are. But I have never personally met anyone in multilevel marketing who has been able to sustain a vibrant, dependent, flourishing relationship with God. I believe this is because of three things.

First, the promotional hype at the core of multilevel marketing causes covetousness.

Second, the system fosters discontent.

Third, the cultlike control involved in MLM causes blind following, not hearing God's voice and doing His will. With network marketing organizations built on worldly desires and entrenched with greed, it would be hard to jump in the water without getting wet.

In *Experiencing God*, authors Blackaby and King compare and contrast God-centered living with self-centered living. They say that God-centered living is characterized by:

- Confidence in God
- Dependence on God and His ability and provision
- Life focused on God and His activity
- Humbleness before God
- Denying self
- Seeking first the kingdom of God and His righteousness
- Seeking God's perspective in every circumstance
- Holy and godly living.[9]

In contrast, self-centered living is characterized by:

- Life focused on self
- Pride in self and self's accomplishments
- Self-confidence
- Depending on self and self's own abilities
- Affirming self
- Seeking to be acceptable to the world and its ways
- Looking at circumstances from a human perspective
- Selfish and ordinary living.[10]

MLM encourages self-centered, not God-centered, living.

Covetousness and discontent have spread like poison through the church. Christian television has shown self-promotion at its worst, with blatant emotional exploitation to obtain money or a following. As long as we refuse to let the Lord deal with our worldly attitudes and heart motives, our fruit will be rotten.

A friend of mine who is an associate pastor was troubled when he heard I was writing this book. Frank and his wife, Flora, have tens of thousands of people in their sales organization selling a high-priced personal-care line. They don't actively recruit people from church, but their lifestyle of new cars, fancy homes, business travel around the country, exotic vacations, and expensive clothes cannot help but be a lure.

Frank tried to tell me that their company was different. He said they don't focus on recruiting but on retailing. and they don't encourage people to recruit at church. When I watched the company video and training material, images of sandy beaches, big houses, and expensive cars flashed across the screen. The video called their business "the opportunity of a lifetime with a stable, secure company . . . not your typical fly-by-night setup, but solid as a rock . . . products you can be proud of and an opportunity to make a significant income by building an organization."

Does this kind of material make people want more money or more of Jesus?

The crux of the problem with most network marketing sales organizations is that in order to build your business, you must use your contacts with friends, family, and acquaintances. Selling something and making a profit isn't wrong. But when you have to recruit everyone you know, using relationships for personal gain to be successful, it is almost impossible to keep pure heart motives.

Statistics show that about 25 percent of those involved in MLM make a profit, 25 percent break even, and 50 percent lose money.[11] In order to succeed, you have to dramatically recruit . . . and then continually recruit to replace the people who quit.

A pastor once sent me an email saying he agreed with my concerns about network marketing. But he assured me that he was a very balanced person and would not get consumed by the opportunity he was planning to enter into. When I wrote him back, I posed some questions. "What will happen when the distributors in your congregation find out you're looking for others to help you in your company? What if some of them become consumed with the money-making focus and walk away from the Lord? Do you want that on your conscience?" As expected, he did not reply.

A main weakness of network marketing is the requirement to produce a team filled with people who are "go-getter, type-A personalities." Something is wrong when you're trained to look for individuals who are compulsive workaholics with no boundaries because they'll go out there and make you money.

Seventy-five percent of direct selling participants in the US in 2020 were women.[12] Network marketing goes right for the heart of the home: the mothers. If you recruit a mom who is trying to stay home with her kids and raise them to know and love God, will she spend so much time on the business that she doesn't have a chance to nurture her children? In many home-based models, the phone starts ringing (or nowadays the texts start flying) at dinnertime and doesn't quit until 9:00 p.m. or later.

Today many pastors, missionaries, and leaders of nonprofit ministries are getting involved in various money-making ventures. They wouldn't be tempted by these schemes if we took better care of those in the ministry by faithfully tithing to the local church, giving additional offerings to reputable ministries, and donating to missionaries who are doing the Lord's work. By our own selfishness, we have forced many men and women of God to seek out other ways to make ends meet.

Great sounding get-rich-quick schemes are offered daily within the body of Christ. Introductory meetings are laced with Scripture verses, and high-profile Christians use their credibility in ministry to back up their claims. Christian leaders and lay people spend incredible amounts of time, resources, and energy chasing great commissions instead of being involved in the Great Commission. They are doing what I was convicted of—preying, not praying.

I recently heard on the radio a man named John tell about going to a hype-filled opportunity meeting. When he asked about the intense focus on making money, the speaker quoted Ecclesiastes 10:19 (NIV): "Money is the answer for everything." He insinuated that if John actually knew the Word of God, he would know better than to ask such a foolish question.

Christians like this take Scripture out of context to justify their actions, leading unsuspecting believers down a path of unrighteousness.

At no time does Satan reveal the consequences of sin. The sin of adultery looks alluring in television dramas. They don't show the destruction it causes, the pain inflicted on everyone involved, the heartbreaking devastation on the children. All you see is the glitter. It appeals to your base senses and leads you gently down the road of spiritual death.

The same thing happens in multilevel marketing. The enemy doesn't want you to hear about all the divorces, bankruptcies, adultery, estranged children, destroyed friendships, and defeated Christians. He only shows you the glitter. No wonder two-thirds of ex-participants in MLM would not join the same or a similar organization again.[13]

The enemy likes to tempt you when you're most vulnerable. He tempted Jesus after He had been fasting for forty days and His body was weak.

Think about the occasions when you've been offered an opportunity that appealed to the lust of the flesh. In what ways were you vulnerable in that moment? Maybe you were low on money and had just heard about coming layoffs, so you were feeling insecure about the future. Whenever fear sets in, watch out! Satan will be right there to tempt you.

A few weeks ago I received what looked like an ordinary chain letter. Someone who claimed to be a sister in the Lord wrote that she and her husband had been praying for a way to get the money to fix their roof. They felt that this "opportunity" was the way that the Lord was providing, saying that "He works in mysterious ways." The letter started out:

> *Dear friends,*
>
> Ordinarily I ignore chain letters, and up to now I have never sent one out. But this is different. It is only to women, and only from one friend to another. We know who we are, and each of us needs money for something worthwhile.
>
> Jill Nelson told me she ran this letter four times last year. The first time she received $10,000 and the other times nearly $7,000.

Recipients were instructed to put a certain amount of money into four envelopes, then send them to the first four names on the attached list, leaving off the top name and adding their own at the bottom.

At the end, it said, "THIS IS NOT AN ILLEGAL CHAIN LETTER."

Really? Just because someone types those words on the bottom of the page, that doesn't make it true.

I wondered if the woman who'd sent it had really prayed about it.

Out of curiosity, I called the attorney general's office to see if it was legal. Of course, it wasn't. What true Christian would think the Lord would provide money by illegal means?

Leaders Gone Astray

I recently received an email from a fellow believer named Dan. He shared his concern over a pastor friend in Alaska who was heavily promoting the granddaddy of all network marketing organizations. When Dan saw him a few months ago for the first time in several years, this pastor only seemed to want to pitch the company, not to fellowship or talk about the Lord.

Herb and Lori had been youth leaders during college. He became an elder and Lori got involved in women's ministries. A couple of years ago, they decided to start attending a different church. Their attendance quickly dropped to the point that one service every two months became the norm. But they regularly contacted members to invite them to come to a business meeting in their home.

When they did go to church, they were usually accompanied by business associates. Herb and Lori directed them to talk with specific church members. Anyone who responded negatively to their pitch was told they had "preconceived misconceptions" about the business and that it was a good Christian business opportunity.

Every family they convinced to join is now too busy attending weekend conventions to make it to church.

Another pastor who was once involved in several networking programs told me the system does severe damage to the body of Christ. "These companies suck the lifeblood of the church away by taking up time, energy, and resources. They misfocus young, impressionable Christians and pervert holy relationships."

Another pastor, Paul, tells me his church is "crawling" with programs that pressure individuals to purchase goods and services out of guilt or compassion for other believers. He feels the main objective is not to sell but to recruit. "I am fed up with the constant invitations to 'parties' for overpriced products and skin-care lines that don't do anything more than what I can find at the store. If the Lord has given a believer such a wonderful gift of persuasion, he should use it to evangelize, not commercialize!"

Hearing God

If we learn to hear God's voice, we will be transformed into what He created us to be. In *Hearing God*, author and pastor Peter Lord lists the traps the enemy sets to keep us from discerning the voice of God and how we can avoid those traps.

> The trap of hurry and busyness—
> You can hear God better when you give Him quality time.
>
> The trap of external distractions—
> Filtering out external distractions will help you focus on what God wants to tell you.
>
> The trap of not recognizing God's voice—

The more you get to know God, the more you recognize His voice.

The trap of our mindset—
You will be more sensitive to God's voice in all situations and among all people if you do not predetermine the most likely place to hear it.

The trap of trying too hard—
By recalling God's faithfulness in the past and his promises of guidance, we can learn to wait patiently for his answers.

The trap of presumption—
It is easy to shift from faith in God to faith in a method or past experience.[14]

Pastor Lord cites the three major snares Satan uses as roadblocks on our walk with Christ:

The snare of rebellion—
The sin of rebellion is a decision to do what you want, not what God wants.

The snare of double-mindedness—
A spiritually double-minded person is an individual who has not made up his mind to do God's will, accept God's advice, or believe God's evaluation, no matter what it may be.

The snare of pretense—

Hypocritical is a word used to describe people who are pretentious. It manifests itself in many ways by Christians who pretend to be right with God when they are not. They hope to impress others with their piety. But their pretense, with a smile or a "Praise the Lord" or "I'm doing fine," goes both manward and Godward.[15]

We must be aware of the enemy's strategy if we are going to successfully live the lives God wants us to. And the only way to live a life pleasing to Him is to hear His voice and obey.

QUESTIONS FOR PERSONAL REFLECTION OR
Small Group Study

1. "The number of lifeless, unproductive, lukewarm Christians is rising at an alarming rate. I believe much of this crisis is due to scores of Christians striving for money and worldly success." Do you believe this bold statement is true? Have you seen such things in your church? How does this affect the ministries in your church? Does it alter a focus on the gospel? How?

2. "If we're not watchful for Satan's deceptive suggestions, we will become lovers of the world instead of the sanctified, set-apart people we are chosen to be." This goes with the previous questions. Do you see a trend in your church, in your social circle, in your business? What can you do about it?

3. "The enemy likes to tempt you when you're most vulnerable. He tempted Jesus after He had been fasting for forty days and His body was weak." Can you articulate where you are most vulnerable to satanic attacks? Are you actively standing against his attacks or are you acting out in a passive manner? Describe your experience.

4. "We must be aware of the enemy's strategy if we are going to successfully live the lives God wants us to. And the only way to live a life pleasing to Him is to hear His voice and obey." How do you guard against the enemy's strategy in your life and in your business? What are you doing to amplify God's voice in your life?

CHAPTER TWELVE

HAVE WE BEEN ROBBED?

My attention has recently been drawn to the book of Hosea. The opening chapters tell the story of Hosea who married a prostitute named Gomer. She repeatedly goes astray, and God keeps telling Hosea to take her back. This is a beautiful message to us of God's heart toward His people. The rest of the book outlines the sinfulness of the nation of Israel, God's punishment, His judgment, and His mercy.

Hosea 4:12 (AMPC) says, "The spirit of harlotry has led them astray and they have played the harlot, withdrawing themselves from subjection to their God." According to BibleTools.org two definitions of *harlotry* are "unfaithfulness" and "idolatry." Could it be that significant numbers of Christians have been sucked into unfaithfulness and idolatry by committing their lives, energies, resources, and affections to a multilevel business opportunity? How many are led astray by becoming consumed with a passion for more money, recognition, and possessions?

When I got involved in network marketing, I was obsessed with building an empire and a secure future. It was the most important thing in my life. For me it was an idol.

We withdraw ourselves from subjection to God when we do what we want to do instead of what He wants us to. We can be inspired by people to do something that seems right, feels good, and gives us a rush of adrenaline. We make decisions based on our common sense or the enticing words of the people training us, then we ask God to bless it.

The Fruits of Being Led Astray

How can we tell if we have been led astray by harlotry? The Scriptures are clear. "Harlotry and wine and new wine take away the heart and the mind and the spiritual understanding" (Hosea 4:11 AMPC).

Without spiritual understanding, we will have a hard time understanding God's Word. The deep things of God will escape us and we will not be growing in the Lord. We will become heartless, unable to love as we once did, lacking compassion and sensitivity to the plights of others. There will be an empty hole where our heart used to be.

Joe was very successful in MLM, but he developed a hard heart toward those plagued with difficulties. He rationalized they were losers and he didn't need to waste his time with them.

"They shall eat and not have enough" read (Hosea 4:10a AMPC). If our hearts are lured away by chasing financial success, we will never be satisfied with what we have. No matter how much we achieve, it will never be sufficient.

Marvin made over $50,000 a month and still wasn't happy. He needed a bigger house, a faster car, more money in the bank, and always had to have a new goal to conquer. No matter how much he had, it was never enough.

"They shall play the harlot and beget no increase" (Hosea 4:10b AMPC). If the spirit of harlotry has led us astray, we will give our affections to other lovers (success) and away from our first love (Jesus). We will experience no increase spiritually, financially, maritally, or intellectually.

Milton and June were committed to their company, believing it to be the answer for their financial future. Although they were living on Milton's limited disability income, they changed every product in their home to the new brand. Even at wholesale, many of the items were 25 to 50 percent more expensive than what they would pay at the store. They spent hundreds of dollars on motivational tapes and books, and they never missed a rally. They could barely afford to put food on the table and clothe their children.

"My people [habitually] ask counsel of their [senseless] wood idols, and their staff [of wood] gives them oracles and instructs them. For the spirit of harlotry has led them astray" (Hosea 4:12 AMPC). When you get into sales and marketing, you listen to the experts in the industry. You ask for wisdom from those who are successful in the business. When Christians take advice and instruction from unbelievers, carnal Christians, or those who are only supportive of those they can make a profit from, they put themselves in a position to be led astray.

John and Linda were all in with their business. They eliminated every friend who didn't follow them into it. For every decision they needed input on, they asked their upline or someone they looked up to in the organization. They even disassociated from family members who were not involved in the business.

Hosea 4:18 says, "Their drink is rebellion." When I was steeped in the pursuit of success, I found it difficult to submit to authority.

I neglected my family and made major decisions without consulting my husband. I didn't want anyone outside the business to tell me what to do.

Hosea 5:4 (AMPC) says, "Their doings will not permit them to return to their God, for the spirit of harlotry is within them and they do not know the Lord [they do not recognize, appreciate, give heed to, or cherish the Lord]." Those consumed by success do not know God's voice, because they have listened for too long to the voice of the world.

Tom was sure his business opportunity had come to him from God. He spent endless hours away from his family and church to make it a success. He started backsliding into unfaithful relationships. Those in his upline enabled his unhealthy behavior. He didn't listen to God's still, small voice. He just assumed what the people on stage were saying must be from the Lord.

"They shall go with their flocks and with their herds to seek the Lord [inquiring for and requiring Him], but they will not find Him; He has withdrawn Himself from them" (Hosea 5:6 AMPC). People bounce from one church to another, from ministry to ministry, sometimes even moving their family from one location to another, trying to seek God but never finding Him.

Brad was consumed with making it in MLM but never had success. Nearly every Sunday, he responded to his church's altar call, where he tearfully petitioned the Lord to meet his needs, bless his business, and give him prosperity. But victory escaped him. He didn't care about what God wanted from him, only what he wanted from God.

Hosea 5:7 says, "They have dealt treacherously with the Lord, for they have begotten pagan children." It breaks my heart to see the children of those consumed by their businesses reject the Lord, turn away, and become rebellious.

"My people are destroyed for lack of knowledge; because you (the priestly nation) have rejected knowledge, I will also reject you that you shall be no priest to Me; seeing you have forgotten the law of your God, I will also forget your children. The more they increased and multiplied [in prosperity and power], the more they sinned against Me; I will change their glory into shame" (Hosea 4:6–7 AMPC). I see this Scripture as a warning to pastors and those in leadership and ministry who are leading many astray by their involvement in the pursuit of success. If they don't wake up, God will change their glory into shame.

A Call to the Church

If we sincerely ask God to teach us to love the things He loves, hate the things He hates, and spend quality time every day seeking His will, the church will be full of on-fire believers who are consumed with Him. If we pray for the Lord to create a desire in us to hunger and thirst after righteousness (not financial success) and make a commitment to only be involved in whatever His will is for our lives, we will see radical change.

When we say, "I'm not moving ahead until I hear from You, Lord," we will be amazed at what happens. Once we get our agendas out of the way, submit to His will and His ways, and depend on Him to provide for our families, our ministries, and our needs (not necessarily our wants), we will see God do creative miracles. I know. I've experienced it.

My prayer for the body of Christ is that we will be sensitive to all the things we are doing that defile the church. That we would be aware of our true heart motives and ask the Lord to purify us. Only then will we see true revival in our hearts, families, churches, and communities.

Oswald Chambers, in *My Utmost for His Highest*, explained this well.

> "And the very God of peace sanctify you wholly."
> (1 Thessalonians 5:23–24 KJV)

> When we pray to be sanctified, are we prepared to face the standard of these verses? We take the term sanctification much too lightly. Are we prepared for what sanctification will cost? It will cost an intense narrowing of all our interests on earth, and an immense broadening of all our interests in God. Sanctification means intense concentration on God's point of view. It means every power of body, soul and spirit chained and kept for God's purpose only. Are we prepared for God to do in us all that He separated us for? And then after His work is done in us, are we prepared to separate ourselves to God even as Jesus did? "For their sakes I sanctify Myself." The reason some of us have not entered into the experience of sanctification is that we have not realized the meaning of sanctification from God's standpoint. Sanctification means being made one with Jesus so that the disposition that ruled Him will rule us. Are we prepared for what that will cost? It will cost everything that is not of God in us.[16]

We must be desperate for God to change us instead of trying to fix our financial circumstances. If we don't let God deal with us, how much we change our surroundings won't matter.

Consider these additional thoughts from Oswald Chambers's *My Utmost for His Highest*:

There are times when you cannot understand why you cannot do what you want to do. When God brings the blank space, see that you do not fill it in, but wait. The blank space may come in order to teach you what sanctification means; or it may come after sanctification to teach you what service means. Never run before God's guidance. If there is the slightest doubt, then He is not guiding. Whenever there is doubt—don't.[17]

Don't Just Do Something. Stand There!

A friend once asked me, "Did you ever wonder why God decided to name us human beings rather than human doings?" I have always been a doing type of person, but God has changed me, so now I can wait for His guidance.

I agree wholeheartedly with Blackaby and King's comments in *Experiencing God*:

> Sometimes individuals and churches are so busy doing things they think will help God accomplish His purpose that He can't get their attention long enough to use them as servants to accomplish what He wants. We often wear ourselves out and accomplish very little of value to the kingdom.
>
> I think God is crying out and shouting to us, "Don't just do something. Stand there! Enter into a love relationship with Me. Get to know Me. Adjust your life to Me. Let Me love you and reveal Myself to you as I work through you."[18]

A New Life

After I left my multilevel business, I watched God strip away my impure motives and wrong thought processes along with the world's way of thinking and looking at things. He miraculously provided day by day, month by month. As Chuck and I faithfully tithed and only got involved in work He had ordained for us, through diligent prayer and confirmation, believing Him even when it didn't make logical sense to us, God blessed us.

We don't live extravagantly. But we earn enough money to pay the bills every month and have extra to give when a need arises. We are able to be involved in ministry when the Lord leads. He is restoring our family. We have normal relationships with people at church. We have no hidden agendas. Oh, what freedom it is minister to those in the body of Christ without any motive other than doing the Lord's will!

God has revolutionized my life, and I am grateful He has allowed me to share the process with you. I'm not proud of my failures. But I love being able to tell you He can deliver you from all your afflictions and set your feet on the Rock too!

God is continuing to work in my life. Walking out the lessons I've learned isn't always easy. I continue to struggle with my relationships with my children. I still tend to spend too much time working and not enough cultivating friendships. I have to force myself to get up an hour before I have to every morning so I can get my heart settled before the Lord and spend quality time with Him, which sets my day on an even keel. Thus far I remain inclined to focus my attention on things that are important to me instead of concentrating on how I can minister to my husband.

But I am learning to live a more balanced life, one that values relationships and God's will above all else. Now I share Chuck's burning hunger to see people saved and set free by the power of God. I want to be sensitive to what the Lord is saying and doing in my life and the lives of others. I no longer spend all my time scheming how I can do something that will prove my worth and importance. I am so full of His love, peace, and acceptance that I don't need to seek recognition from others. He has truly revolutionized my life. And as I yield myself, my rights, my hopes, my plans, and my will to Him, He continues to transform me day by day.

For years I was consumed with money, prestige, and recognition, leaving me empty at the top. Now I have chosen for my life to be filled by the holy fire of God, His Spirit, and His will. The result of that choice has been restored relationships, pure heart motives, a renewed family life full of depth and dimension, and a vital, energizing, zealous love relationship with the Living God.

A Call to Return to Our First Love

I pray that my experiences will draw you to return to your first love. In Revelation 2:4, God says, "I have this against you, that you have left your first love."

Can you recall what it was like the first time you fell in love? I remember how I acted when that happened to me.

> Whenever I looked at him, I had to catch my breath.
>
> I woke up every morning thinking about him and drifted off to sleep at night doing the same thing.
>
> His presence flooded my mind every waking minute of the day. When I was with him, I didn't want to leave. When I was away from him, I couldn't wait to see him again.
>
> I was always thinking of new ways to fix myself up to please him.

I daydreamed about our future together.

I memorized every detail of his face.

I doodled his name on my notepad and then signed his last name after mine.

I had an intense desire to know everything about him.

I wanted all my friends to meet him.

He became far more important than my friends or other activities in my life.

We spent hours on end just being together and sharing our lives.

When I asked Chuck to think back on his first love, he shared from his perspective.

He changed his schedule so he could see her more often.

He did things he wouldn't ordinarily do because she wanted to.

He found out what kind of clothes and cologne she liked, then wore the things that pleased her.

He gave up going out with the boys to spend time with her.

He spent a lot of money buying her silly things like flowers, trinkets, and cards.

He wrote love poems and love letters.

As I looked over our lists, my heart cried out in repentance to the Lord. "Oh, God, forgive me for not loving You that way! For not giving You my whole heart. Help me to treat You the same way I did my first love. For You alone are worthy of that kind of love and deserving of that level of adoration."

The words of the following song express my deep feelings about taking time with God.

THE HEART OF THE MATTER
Words and Music by Tim Pedigo (used by permission)

You wake up in the morning, crawl out of bed.
Gotta get moving but your heartbeat says,
Oh, take a little time out. You're in a hurry.
Gotta make a little more pay.
Gotta keep the schedule. No time to pray.
Oh, too busy rushin' about.

But the matter at hand
Is what's wrong with your heart.
You lose the battle before you start.
Then the holy flame dies out within
And your spiritual eyes
Grow sadly dim.
You trust yourself
Instead of looking to Him.

Oh, my friend, that's the heart of the matter.

You're hardly out the door
When you encounter the foe.
Walls start fallin' like dominoes.
Oh, but there's still a way out,
Though you're caught up
in the rubble
Of a man-made plan
And you realize things are
out of hand.
Oh, you've gotta take time out.

But the matter at hand
Is what's wrong with your heart.
You lose the battle before you start.
Then the holy flame dies out within
And your spiritual eyes
Grow sadly dim.
You trust yourself
Instead of looking to Him.
Oh, my friend, that's the heart of
the matter.

Your head hits the pillow
As the day draws in,
Battered, defeated, and
alone again.
Oh, a little voice cries out.
Oh, take a little time out.

QUESTIONS FOR PERSONAL REFLECTION OR
Small Group Study

1. "How many are led astray by becoming consumed with a passion for more money, recognition, and possessions?" Have you been led astray by personal passions? You are not alone. Are you brave enough to speak these passions aloud and repent of them? Once you admit these unholy passions, tell someone and have them hold you accountable.

2. "Without spiritual understanding, we will have a hard time understanding God's Word. The deep things of God will escape us, and we will not be growing in the Lord." What are you doing to increase understanding of God's Word? How does this look in your life? Does anyone else see your efforts? Describe the process and the result.

3. "If our hearts are lured away by chasing financial success, we will never be satisfied with what we have. No matter how much we achieve, it will never be sufficient." What are you searching for to bring satisfaction in your life and business? Are you willing to depend on God's sufficiency in your life? Are you seeking Him daily? Will you commit to it today?

4. "Nearly every Sunday, he responded to his church's altar call, where he tearfully petitioned the Lord to meet his needs, bless his business, and give him prosperity. But victory escaped him. He didn't care about what God wanted from him, only what he wanted from God." Do you see this pattern in your life where you consistently ask God to bless and provide for your needs? What would it look like to shift your prayers and ask God what He wants from you? Read Matthew 22:37-39 and discover what God is asking of you.

5. "We take the term sanctification much too lightly. Are we prepared for what sanctification will cost?" Sanctification is the process of growing to become more like Jesus. Where are you currently experiencing God sanctifying you? Are you willing to step into this process of transformation in every area of your life even if it's painful? Our sanctification will not be complete until glory. But until then we can live in anticipation of read I John 3:2 (ESV), "Beloved, we are God's children now, and what we will be has not yet appeared; but we know that when he appears we shall be like him, because we shall see him as he is."

CHAPTER THIRTEEN

YOU CAN BE FREE FROM THE TRAP

One sign of an emotionally healthy person is that he or she is open to new information and other opinions. It is dangerous to be so closed-minded that you never receive other viewpoints or input. In fact, that is how many people become trapped by cults.

When I was ensnared in Scientology, I was convinced it was right for everyone. I was not open to differing opinions. When I noticed things that weren't quite right, I ignored the discrepancies, because I feared losing my friends and support system if I doubted the organization. I didn't allow myself to hear any ideas that opposed my beliefs. While I didn't realize it at the time, fear kept me in captivity.

In *The Kingdom of the Cults*, author Walter Martin states, "First and foremost, the belief systems of the cults are characterized by closed-mindedness. They are not interested in rational cognitive evaluation of the facts."[19]

It is also easy to be convinced about a business opportunity to the point of unhealthy closed-mindedness. Especially if you've built your world around your opportunity. Breaking free from the trap may seem scary, but pray fervently, stay open-minded, and see what the Lord might be trying to say to your heart.

Are you, or someone you love, trapped in the web of striving for financial success? If you're not sure, take this Heart Checkup. Answer the questions as honestly as you can. (If you have a loved one you're concerned about, answer the questions about him or her from your perspective.)

HEART CHECKUP

	YES	NO
Do you spend more time each day thinking about how to build your business than you do the Lord?	☐	☐
Do you view friends, family, and acquaintances as a means to an end (i.e., your success in business)?	☐	☐
Do you consider any negative comments about your product or opportunity as a scheme from the devil to steal your dream?	☐	☐
Do you believe your opportunity is the best way for anyone who wants to earn extra money to fulfill that desire?	☐	☐
Do you talk more about your product or opportunity than you do the things of God?	☐	☐

	Yes	No

Are you more excited, animated, talkative, and enthusiastic about your business than telling a friend about Jesus? ☐ ☐

Do you fellowship exclusively with those who are involved in and/or positive about your business? ☐ ☐

Are you frustrated, angry, even a little bitter with your current employment situation? Do you see this business opportunity as a way of escape from the bondage of your 9-to-5 job? ☐ ☐

Are you convinced that you owe it to your friends and family to share your business opportunity with them? ☐ ☐

Do your role models focus on big incomes, nice houses, new cars, annual vacations, and financial independence? ☐ ☐

Do you tend to concentrate your time and energy on relationships that help you build your business? ☐ ☐

Do you justify pouring resources you don't have into your business because you're confident it will pay off in the long run? ☐ ☐

If you have more than five *yes* answers, you (or your loved one) are trapped in the unhealthy pursuit of monetary success.

How to Break Free

You can find release from the unhealthy pursuit of success at any cost. It may not be easy. The Lord might need to do a major overhaul on the values you hold and the way you view the circumstances in your life. Be open to His direction, willing to admit that you don't know what's best for you like Jesus does.

Only when we are completely yielded to the Lord can He accomplish His perfect will in our lives. When He does that, we are truly successful!

Start now by choosing to walk in these steps to freedom:

1. Admit that you've made a mistake in getting involved in this business venture. "There is a way that seems right to a man, but its end is the way of death" (Proverbs 14:12 ESV).
2. Ask God to help you discern His voice above all others. Commit yourself to listening to Him and being obedient. Read *Hearing God* by Peter Lord. "The gatekeeper opens the gate for him, and the sheep recognize his voice and come to him. He calls his own sheep by name and leads them out" (John 10:3 NLT).
3. Ask God to show you your heart as He sees it: the bad as well as the good. "Search me, O God, and know my heart; try me, and know my anxieties; and see if there is any wicked way in me, and lead me in the way everlasting" (Psalms 139:23–24).
4. Ask God to enable you to love the things He loves and hate the things He hates. Pray that He will break you, change you, purify you, cleanse you. "Create in me a clean heart, O God, and renew a steadfast spirit within me" (Psalms 51:10).
5. Allow the Lord to convict your soul, especially in the areas of your motives and the idolatry of being consumed by success

instead of Jesus. Write down everything He reveals to you. "The heart is deceitful above all things, and desperately wicked; who can know it? I, the Lord, search the heart, I test the mind, even to give every man according to his ways, and according to the fruit of his doings" (Jeremiah 17:9–10).

6. Confess to the Lord the sins you wrote down. Repent (which means turn away from those sins) and ask Him to forgive you. "If we confess our sins, He is faithful and just to forgive us our sins and to cleanse us from all unrighteousness" (1 John 1:9).

7. Ask the Lord if there are unresolved issues in your life that have driven you to seek comfort in your business. If He shows you some areas of wounding or abuse, ask Him to heal your heart and trust that He will tenderly do so. If more help is needed, seek out Bible-based Christian counseling or a support group to help you work through your issues. "He heals the brokenhearted and binds up their wounds" (Psalms 147:3).

8. Pray for discernment and godly wisdom. Take authority over double-mindedness in the name of Jesus. "If any of you lacks wisdom, let him ask of God, who gives to all liberally and without reproach, and it will be given to him. But let him ask in faith, with no doubting, for he who doubts is like a wave of the sea driven and tossed by the wind. For let not that man suppose that he will receive anything from the Lord; he is a double-minded man, unstable in all his ways" (James 1:5–8).

9. Make a conscious effort to surround yourself with people who are hungry for more of God. Meet regularly with other Christians. Ask God to send you a prayer partner. Learn how

to establish healthy boundaries in relationships, work, and life. "The righteous should choose his friends carefully. For the way of the wicked leads them astray" (Proverbs 12:26).

10. Surrender yourself completely to Jesus. Pray, "Have Your way, Lord!" Set aside all personal agendas and tell the Lord you want His perfect will for your life. Read *Experiencing God: How to Live the Full Adventure of Knowing and Doing the Will of God* by Henry T. Blackaby and Claude V. King. "Teach me to do Your will, for You are my God; Your Spirit is good. Lead me in the land of uprightness. Revive me, O Lord, for Your name's sake! For Your righteousness' sake bring my soul out of trouble" (Psalms 143:10–11).

11. Be willing to give up, walk away from, and die to your will, your plans, your agenda. "Most assuredly, I say to you, unless a grain of wheat falls into the ground and dies, it remains alone; but if it dies, it produces much grain. He who loves his life will lose it, and he who hates his life in this world will keep it for eternal life. If anyone serves Me, let him follow Me; and where I am, there My servant will be also. If anyone serves Me, him My Father will honor" (John 12:24–26).

12. Ask God to show you His desires for for your life, how He enjoys watching you use the gifts and talents He gave you. "Commit your works to the Lord, and your thoughts will be established" (Proverbs 16:3).

13. Be obedient to what He tells you, no matter how ridiculous it may seem. "Let this mind be in you which was also in Christ Jesus, who, being in the form of God, did not consider it robbery to be equal with God, but made Himself of no reputation, taking the form of a bondservant, and coming in the likeness of men. And being found in appearance as

a man, He humbled Himself and became obedient to the point of death, even the death of the cross" (Philippians 2:5–8).

These steps may take weeks, months, or even years to master, but the Lord will use them to soften your heart to His will and His ways. Be open to His guiding and confirmation as you walk through to freedom.

Be careful not to grow bitter toward those who have knowingly or unknowingly set traps for you in business (Psalms 140:5). Many people who inspire others by using the ways of the world aren't even aware they are doing so. Ask the Lord to help you have a forgiving heart. Then make a firm decision not to become offended at what others have done to you. Forgive them, for they know not what they do.

I will even go a step further to say it might be worth asking God, *What do I need to own in this spiritual detour?* You might find out your unhealed trauma made you vulnerable to the deception of MLM.

How to Repair Flawed Relationships

Now that you've seen the harm you've caused to the connections in your life, it is important that you reconcile them through repentance and by asking forgiveness wherever possible. Here are a few steps to consider.

1. Prayerfully create a list of those you've harmed in building your business. Ask the Lord to bring names to your mind.
2. Write out exactly how you've hurt them.
   For example: In my pursuit to be successful, I focused on using all my personal relationships to make money. I called

_____ on the phone and tried to rebuild our friendship with the hidden motive to recruit him or her into my business. This action devalued _____ as a person.

or

In my enthusiasm to build my business, I used tactics that were not completely aboveboard. In fact, they were downright deceitful. In order to recruit _____, I had to tell half-truths, and I got to the point where I believed the lies. Being dishonest in my communication with _____ defiled our relationship.

3. If possible, go to the person you sinned against. Admit your wrong, confess your sin, and ask him or her to forgive you for misusing the relationship.
4. Make a personal commitment to the Lord to keep pure heart motives for all future relationships.

How to Help Others Break Free

The most important thing you can do to assist others find freedom from being consumed by success is pray. Ask God to soften their hearts and enable them to be open to the truth. Your most powerful resource is prayer.

The Challenge

Are you at a crossroads where you want to lay aside ungodly practices to make money and using people to succeed but are still attracted by the lure of easy money or motivated by financial success? If so, I say to you, "Choose this day whom you will serve" (Joshua 24:15 ESV).

Your choice will make a difference for eternity.

QUESTIONS FOR PERSONAL REFLECTION OR *Small Group Study*

1. "One sign of an emotionally healthy person is that he or she is open to new information and other opinions." Who is in your circle that you trust to listen to their opinion and instruction? Are you serious about learning God's way of living? How does this look in your business?

2. "You can find release from the unhealthy pursuit of success at any cost. It may not be easy. The Lord might need to do a major overhaul on the values you hold and the way you view the circumstances in your life." Does this process scare you? What could you lose if you allowed God to make these changes?

3. Are you willing to make the effort with God's help? Can you trust God with this area of your life and business? Take time to pray through this process and share your need with someone who will encourage you to trust the Lord.

CHAPTER FOURTEEN

THE NARROW WAY

After the initial printing of *Consumed by Success*, I did scores of radio and TV interviews . . . and no doubt made more than a few dyed-in-the-wool believers in MLM angry. But many people called into these programs or wrote me later saying, "I always knew there was something wrong with multilevel marketing but I could never put my finger on it. You are the first person I've ever heard verbalize what I was feeling. Thank you!"

When I did the *Prime Time America* show on the Moody Network with Jim Warren, a pastor called in and shared that he had been involved in two MLM programs and had almost missed his ministry calling.

When I was on the *Andy Anderson Live!* Show, a woman called in and shared that her four-year-old daughter told her, "Mommy, you love money more than you love me." In that moment this mother knew she had to walk away from the whole thing.

Some people who had made it to the top in MLM and then slowed down long enough to hear God's voice have reported to me, "What you are saying is so true!" Many have shared that God spoke the same things to them and led them to repentance.

Majoring in the Minors

Those who are committed to the "success system" of MLM and are actively building momentum don't want to hear what I'm saying. They have too much to protect. Or they have blinders on and are unwilling to entertain the thought that God might be speaking to them. Many of those I am upsetting with my message say things like "Oh, she just had a bad experience. If she were with my company, she would feel differently about MLM" or "Only people who are workaholics like Athena would have a problem with MLM, so her message is not for me." They don't want to hear the truth, so they major in the minors and miss the whole intention.

My message has nothing to do with specific companies or products. There are good companies and bad ones, good products and bad. We need to examine our heart motives as well as how the opportunity to make big money affects our spiritual lives.

The problems I encountered in MLM do not relate only to those who tend to be type-A personalities. It's just easier for people like me to get out of balance. The subtle mind-altering philosophies that encourage us to covet what others have and become discontent with what we have affects everyone involved in MLM. And yes, I said *everyone.*

On an hour-long radio program in Alabama, almost all the callers agreed with what I was saying and shared their experiences of being solicited in church and feeling used and defiled. The host supported what I was saying, even confronting one caller who tried to justify his involvement in MLM. Within twenty-four hours the largest distributor for the most well-known MLM company in the country called the station and threatened to stop supporting the station if they didn't destroy the tape of our interview and get rid of the host! Within thirty days, the host was fired. It turned out the entire radio staff was steeped in various MLM programs to fund the station budget. They certainly didn't want to hear what I had to say!

Almost invariably, someone will call in and say many people are being saved through their company who, if not for their opportunity, wouldn't have come to know the Lord. I used to buy into that rationale. I convinced myself that because people in our business got saved at a company function, what I did was "of God." We sales-types are always looking for something that will give us and our products or services credibility. And after all, my upline led me to the Lord, as did Chuck's. We had every reason to believe MLM had some redeeming value. But you've heard the story of Balaam in Numbers 22–24, right? If God can use a donkey, he can use an MLM to get someone's attention.

The Lord has shown me He can certainly use a company, or someone in that company, to bring someone to the point of salvation. But that doesn't make the company great—it makes Him great! He is the one who should be praised and glorified, not the company. First Corinthians 3:6–7 says, "I planted, Apollos watered, but God gave the increase. So then neither he who plants is anything, nor he who waters, but God who gives the increase."

When I recently saw the founder of a large MLM company on the cover of a well-known Christian magazine, I was deeply concerned. The interview painted a wonderful picture of this man and all the money he donates to ministries—all of which I'm sure is true. The founder provided credibility that well-meaning Christians could use to recruit other Christians into their downline. The more examples of "spiritual success" they have to make potential recruits ignore any red flags, the better they will be at reeling in followers of Jesus.

When I appeared on a national TV show, the couple who interviewed me mentioned their hesitation toward having me on since so many of their supporters were involved in MLM. Every time I zeroed in on MLM, the host made qualifying statements like "But that could be true about involvement in any kind of business."

As I pondered his comment, the Lord showed me the error in that thinking. Only MLM has the philosophy of recruiting a part-time army of distributors where anyone with a hundred dollars or so can get involved. Since just about everyone is a prospect, this has the potential for a widespread effect on the church. If someone were consumed by their real estate career or their climb up the corporate ladder (or their ministry for that matter), he or she wouldn't be on the lookout for scores and scores of recruits with whom to build their business. People who have a thriving law practice aren't consumed with a passion to inspire others to do the same and help them do so.

Some callers say, "I have my MLM business under control. I'm totally balanced and keep my priorities in order." I suggest they consider 1 Corinthians 8:9, which says, "Beware lest somehow this liberty of yours become a stumbling block to those who are weak." If you are convincing other people to get involved, you never know when a weaker brother or sister is going to be destroyed by the love of money and completely walk away from the Lord.

When I was on *Money Matters with Larry Burkett*, he shared the following:

> I have said many times, there's nothing fundamentally wrong with MLM—the difficulty is the motivation involved. What I have seen is that very few people are able to control that motivation, because more money breeds more money; and maybe more insidious than that, it breeds success—that feeling that I'm worth something to somebody other than my

family and God. Receiving all that recognition and accolades can be a very dangerous thing.

What Athena tells in a real way in her story is what I saw in a real way in an awful lot of the people I counseled back in the '70s and '80s. Typically, what I would see was one of the spouses—usually the more exuberant of the two—would get involved in an MLM program. They would then draw in the other spouse, because the company would encourage couples to "build the business" together. Immediately, it ended up drawing them both away from their family. Almost invariably, one of the two spouses, more often than not the husband, would drop out, realizing he really didn't want to leave his job or change careers. The wife would stay involved, but now he would be taking care of the kids in the evenings while she attended motivational meetings and sales conferences. She would grow further and further estranged from him and would rationalize it by saying, "We need the money. You're really not providing enough income for us to have the home or car we should have." I saw many, many marriages destroyed—not because of MLM, but because they couldn't keep their motivation straight."[20]

His advice to his listeners regarding MLM was this:

First: Know what God has called you to do and be sure you are doing that, whatever it is.

Second: Be a good steward. Before you need any more money, you need to be a better steward of the money you already have. We have proved many times in the past with numerous couples that more money won't help their problem—in fact, it only feeds the problem.

Third: If you're going to get involved, keep your recruiting efforts out of your church. I resigned my membership from a church once because the Sunday my wife and I stood up to join the church, three people solicited me in the lobby for different MLM programs. I thought to myself, *Boy, if the church leadership doesn't have that under control, they don't have anything under control!*

Fourth: If your bent in life is toward success and money and motivation, you need to flee these programs. They will destroy your life, they will destroy your family, and they will destroy your relationship with God."[21]

MLM has been called "the wave of the future" by business experts. Yes, it is a good way for a company to get its product into the hands of consumers. But is it really good for those involved? I say, emphatically, no. If we bring people into a situation where they are tempted and even encouraged to run after the things of the world, I liken it to contributing to the delinquency of a believer. The enemy can use even seemingly good things to distract us from God's true plan for our lives.

As Christians, can we persist in going down that wide road that leads to destruction? If we flirt with the world, we will fall into the category of those Jesus mentions in Revelation 3:17 who say they are rich but are really "wretched, miserable, poor, blind, and naked." Instead, we are called to take up our cross and follow Jesus.

Jesus calls us to say no to those things that would feed the lust of the flesh, the lust of the eyes, and the pride of life (1 John 2:16). We are to live our lives without compromise, justifying our sin, or abusing the grace that is ours. We must be quick to repent, to "walk in the light as He is in the light" (1 John 1:7), to be so sensitive to the Holy Spirit that we immediately know when we are out of line. The narrow way charges us to not just say we love God but to prove it by obeying all of His commands.

QUESTIONS FOR PERSONAL REFLECTION OR
Small Group Study

1. "We need to examine our heart motives as well as how the opportunity to make big money affects our spiritual lives." Have you examined your heart concerning the dream you are chasing?

2. Larry Burkett: "Know what God has called you to do and be sure you are doing that, whatever it is." This is a lifetime challenge that encompasses your business, your ministry, and your life. Are you actively doing what God has called you to do in these three areas? If not, are you willing to step into His calling? How can you begin to make this shift in your business, your ministry, and your life?

3. "The narrow way charges us to not just say we love God but to prove it by obeying all of His commands." This is the heart of the matter. We aren't saved by following His commands, but those of us who are saved are required to deny ourselves and take up our cross daily. Not easy to do. Are you willing to actively and intentionally obey His commands? Where do you see this could be a struggle in regard to your business? What part of your business do you need to surrender to Him?

EPILOGUE

Nearly thirty years ago I printed the first one thousand copies of this book. You would think in all that time things would have changed, but they haven't. The MLM industry has only altered its tactics. Now, instead of opportunity meetings, there are webinars, conference calls, Zoom calls, and predatory strategies on social media. Distributors and coaches are being trained to go into Facebook groups with people who are struggling with lifelong illnesses, target them, befriend them, and ensnare them. Misusing the platform by friending people you don't know in order to sell them something is disgraceful, deceptive, and just plain wrong.

The same greed and power I saw ruling and reigning in MLM when I was in the inner circle is still in charge today. Companies lure people in with promises of answers to all their problems and don't care about delivering on what they offer. If you go to YouTube and type "anti MLM" in the search bar, you'll hear from all sorts of people who've made it to the top and then walked away for good.

Because of the way it perverts motives and focuses on the things of this world, I believe the MLM model is unredeemable. I don't see how any Christian can, in good conscience, be involved. But I certainly understand how so many get manipulated into it. It's hard to guard your heart when you've been deceived into thinking the opportunity you bought into is an answer to prayer.

Once you buy into the lie, MLM preys on your vulnerability, baits you into selling your soul for riches and power. Just like a cult, they groom you, manipulate you, and teach you to shame and intimidate others into not speaking up or questioning their behavior. All the while, they dangle the carrot of financial freedom in front of you, just far enough out of your reach so you never get it but keep trying. The business model and its methods are emotionally, mentally, and spiritually abusive. You may be fooled into justifying it as a way to get what you think is God's best for you, but nothing could be further from the truth.

Vulnerable to Deception

When the Lord gave me insight into PTSD and how the wounds caused by trauma in our past can control us, I sensed God's call to share what I learned with other women who'd been deceived by MLM. I encouraged women to let God into those places of pain that had never been healed and find the restoration He wanted to bring.

It's easy to think, since we are a new creation, we never have to look back and receive healing for past wounds. The truth is, while our spirit is new, our places of pain still need redemption.

But even after He opened my eyes to and set me free from my bondage, I still did not apply what I discovered to my own wounds. As I avoided going back to my painful childhood and allowing Jesus in to bring emotional health, I was left vulnerable to deception.

Five years after this book was originally published, I was introduced to a pastor's wife at an extremely credible Christian writers' conference. Chuck and I brought this couple into our lives in a leadership role that resulted in almost thirteen years of spiritual abuse. During that time I lost my marriage, my family, most of my friends, my twenty-year-old, $3.5 million publishing company, my house, my credit rating, and my reputation. I almost my faith.

When I finally walked away from that experience, I asked God, *What in the world just happened?* How could I have believed a lie and given up everything for it, believing it was God's will for me, only to find out I'd been conned and deceived? *Lord, how could that kind of deception befall a professing Christian?*

His answer held conviction. "Athena, your unhealed wounding left you vulnerable to deception." Godly sorry filled my heart as I took in that difficult truth.

The untended-to areas in my heart caused me to be open to Scriptures being taken out of context, manipulation, shaming, shunning, and a shutting down of my ability to reason by the Spirit and in truth.

First God delivered me from the deception of MLM, and then once again God faithfully redeemed and restored me after thirteen years of spiritual abuse and the deception it entailed. Two years after walking away from the spiritual abuse that defined who I was, He put me back into publishing. I now use my gifts in the business sector in a way that honors Him.

As the Holy Spirit helps me to zoom out and connect the dots, I see scores of broken and wounded Christian women who are being taken in by a scheme of the enemy through this MLM business model, convinced it is an answer to their prayers and God's will for them.

I believe the Lord wants to use His children to glorify His name in various creative styles, but never in a way that ends up with us feeling empty at the top. He will provide for us in amazing ways that can only point to Him so we can be examples of His faithfulness in ways that truly bring transformation to others.

May it ever be so.

QUESTIONS FOR PERSONAL REFLECTION OR *Small Group Study*

1. "'Your unhealed wounding left you vulnerable to deception.' Godly sorry filled my heart as I took in that difficult truth." Do you have unhealed wounds in your life? God wants to completely heal them, but the healing process is not usually easy or without pain. Are you willing to let God heal you, whatever the cost? Prayerfully consider the wounds in your life that need healing. As you close this book don't shut out the prompting of the Spirit as He is bringing awareness to these wounds. Take the time to heal and to repent of anything that would leave you open to deception. When you do you will discover a renewed freedom in what God is calling you to do and you will see His blessings in your life. Blessings that are completely different that those you previously longed for.

2. The difference you will experience is quite a contrast from where we began. Instead of finding yourself "Empty at the Top" you will bask in the goodness of our God as you are filled to the brim within your humble surrender. And that, my friend, is a place where He will take your big dreams and multiply them for the Kingdom!

ENDNOTES

Chapter Seven
1. Lord, Peter, *Hearing God* (Grand Rapids, MI: Chosen 2011), pp. 171-172.

Chapter Nine
2. Gothard, Bill, *Men's Manual, Volume II - Financial Freedom* (Oak Brook, IL: Institute In Basic Youth Conflicts, 1983), pp. 22-25.
3. Ibid., p. 23.
4. Ibid., p. 105.
5. Ibid., p. 105.
6. Ibid., pp. 106-109.

Chapter Ten
7. Waite, Maurice, *Pocket Oxford American Dictionary & Thesaurus* (Oxford University Press, 2010), p. 773.
8. https://www.dictionary.com/browse/purpose.

Chapter Eleven
9. Blackaby, King, *Experiencing God* (Nashville, TN: Broadman & Holman, 1994), pp. 63-64.
10. Ibid, p. 64.
11. Branka, "MLM Statistics – 2023," July 1, 2023, https://truelist.co/blog/mlm-statistics.

[12] Ibid.
[13] Ibid.
[14] Lord, Peter, *Hearing God* (Grand Rapids, MI: Chosen, 2011), pp. 99-105.
[15] Lord, Peter, pp. 113-119.

Chapter Twelve
[16] Chambers, Oswald, *My Utmost for His Highest* (Westwood, NJ: Barbour and Company, 1963), p. 39.
[17] Chambers, Oswald, *My Utmost for His Highest* (Westwood, NJ: Barbour and Company, 1963), p. 4.
[18] Blackaby, King, *Experiencing God* (Nashville, TN: Broadman & Holman, 1994), p. 19.

Chapter Thirteen
[19] Martin, Walter, *The Kingdom of the Cults* (Minneapolis, MN: Bethany House Publishers, 1985), p. 26.

Chapter Fourteen
[20] Burkett, Larry, *Money Matters* (Gainesville, GA: Christian Financial Concepts, 1996), live radio broadcast, April 23, 1996.
[21] Burkett, Larry, *Money Matters* (Gainesville, GA: Christian Financial Concepts, 1996), live radio broadcast, April 23, 1996.

SUGGESTED READING

Blackaby and King. *Experiencing God*. Nashville, TN: Broadman & Holman, 1994.

Bridges, Jerry. *The Pursuit of Holiness*. Colorado Springs, CO: NavPress, 1978.

Dortch, Richard. *Fatal Conceit*. Green Forest, AR: New Leaf Press, 1993.

Gothard, Bill. *Men's Manual, Volume II—Financial Freedom*. Oak Brook, IL: Institute in Basic Youth Conflicts, 1983.

Hemfelt, Robert, Frank Minirth, and Paul Meier. *1# Are Driven: The Compulsive Behaviors America Applauds*. Nashville, TN: Thomas Nelson Publishers, 1991.

Lord, Peter. *Hearing God (Revised & Expanded)*. Grand Rapids, MI: Chosen, 2011.

Perkins, Bill. *Fatal Attractions: Overcoming Our Secret Addictions*. Eugene, OR: Harvest House Publishers, 1991.

Seamands, David. *Freedom from the Performance Trap*. Wheaton, IL: Victor Books, 1988.

Wilkerson, David. *Hungry for More of Jesus*. Grand Rapids, MI: Chosen Books, 1992.

OTHER RESOURCES BY ATHENA DEAN HOLTZ

Full Circle: Coming Home to the Faithfulness of God

Together for a Purpose: Love and Mission in Marriage and Ministry

Redeemed & Restored Blog

Redeemed & Restored YouTube Channel

All Things Podcast

If you have a story of MLM abuse,
I'd love to hear from you and learn
how you discovered it and are healing from it.
Visit mlmabuse.com
and contact me from there.

In an attempt to help you begin the journey into yielding to the Lord in business, in ministry, in your marriage or relationships, I offer you this commitment. This is the kind of announcement God LOVES to help you walk out! And He will!

COMMITMENT TO SURRENDER

With God's help I will commit myself to live my life in honesty and truth, completely surrendered to His will and His ways.

> I will acknowledge my faults and ask forgiveness.
> I will seek help when I need it.
> I will commit myself to learning to hear God's voice and then,
> by His grace, obey what I hear.
> I will return to my first love.

_____

Your signature

_____

Date

To order additional copies of this book, contact:
Redemption Press
1602 Cole Street
Enumclaw, WA 98022
www.redemption-press.com

For quantity discount information or to place an order by phone, call (360) 226-3488.

All author royalties have been donated to nonprofit ministries and missionaries in the US and Canada.

ORDER INFORMATION

To order additional copies of this book, please visit
www.redemption-press.com.
Also available at Christian bookstores, Amazon, and Barnes and Noble.

www.ingramcontent.com/pod-product-compliance
Lightning Source LLC
Chambersburg PA
CBHW031629210526
45464CB00004B/1814